MARY'S ...
A PERFECT MODEL OF FAITH EXPRESSION (LUKE 1:46-56)

REV FATHER AARON AGBESHIE AGORSOR

WEBSITE: www.fatheraaron.org

EMAIL: aaron@fatheraaron.org

ISBN: 9798632429122

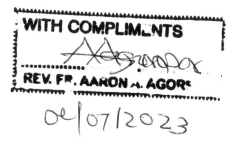

WITH COMPLIMENTS

REV. FR. AARON A. AGOR...

04/07/2023

DEDICATION

I dedicate this book to my parents, my siblings,
my benefactors and all through whose help I
have become a priest.

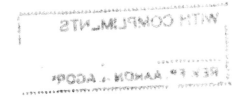

2

CONTENTS

ACKNOWLEDGMENTS

Anyone who seeks the truth must learn to show gratitude; must be grateful. Taking cognisance of the fact that had it not been God, I would not have become a priest, I wish to thank Him for his unmerited favour, the gift and the joy of the Priesthood. My next gratitude goes to my Archbishop, Most Rev. Charles Gabriel Palmer-Buckle, Metropolitan Archbishop of Accra, for his encouragement and support. When I first posted this piece on Facebook, he read it and remarked to me, "You are a strong Mariologist; keep it up my son!"

I thank, also, my parents Mr. Brummel Hugh Yao Agorsor and Miss Rebecca Abotsi and my siblings Yayra, Mawukoenya, Tsoeke, and Nyatefe who have been my bedrock and my joy ever since I began my formation to the Priesthood. Special mention is made of my brother, Tsoeke and his wife Affi for their encouragement and support. You sacrificed even your last penny for me when times were hard. When it was obvious that as a graduate, I was supposed to contribute my quota to the growth of the family and I made the choice of the Priesthood, you stood by me and single-handedly shouldered the burdens of the family. You are my greatest benefactors.

To my loving benefactors, Mr. & Mrs. Nicol, you are my sunshine because you came into my life at a time when I was almost giving up on my formation. You did not only support financially, you prayed with and for me. I cannot forget Mr. & Mrs. Ahulu, Mr & Mrs Esiape, Dr. & Mrs Aglobitse, Mrs Doris Tay, Madam Joana Ampofo, Mr. & Mrs Agyirakwah, the Ashigbey family, Honourable & Mrs. Humado, Mr & Mrs. Vanlare Dosoo, Mr. & Mrs Asante-Antwi, Miss Adjongba-Sik, Mrs Florence Dweben, Robert Nyaku, Mr. & MrsAdane-Mensah, Mr. & Mrs Danquah, Michael Funtror, Barrister Hugh Marcel Potakey, Mr. & Mrs Awusu, Mr. & Mrs Opoku, Mr. & Mrs Amponsah, Mr. & Mrs Yamoah, Mr. & Mrs. Komla, Mr. & Mrs Tettey, Mr. & Mrs Akondor, Mr. & Mrs Ashun, Mr. & Mrs Cobbinah, Mrs Kwawukume, Mrs Adadevoh Alphonse Bulloro, Albert Apewe, Donatus Pallu, Bernard Sor, Dr. Etse Sikanku, Mr. & Mrs Kwachie and Miss Elizabeth Aggrey.

I cannot forget the many priests who journeyed with me especially Rev. Frs. Joseph Blay OFM, Michael Kodzo Mensah, Ebenezer Akesseh, John Neuman Tettehfio, Richmond Dzekoe, Samuel Korkordi, Dennis Opoku, Donald Hinfey S. J, my Spiritual Director in the Seminary, Clement Wilson, Baffour Akowuah, Francis Asagba, Koos Janssen, SMA, Gabriel Kojovi Liashiedzi, my Parish Priest, Rev. Monsignor James Robert Myers, and Rev. Monsignor Jonathan Ankrah.

To my classmates in the ministry, Rev. Frs. Michael Melvin Mensah, Emmanuel Codjoe, Emmanuel Salifu, Hillary Agbenosi, Lawrence Agyepong, Osmond Kudoloh, and Gabriel Ettiene,

I thank you for the beautiful times we spent together in the seminary. It is an added impetus to my own formation. Let us stay connected always!

Finally, seldom is a piece of printing the result of one efforts-nor is this book you now hold. The author would like to tender a special word of thanks to Mrs Uzo Agyare-Kumi, Edem Kobla Gavor, Michael Yamoah and Stephen Sanniez Owora Asare, who painstakingly edited this material for me. May God reward them abundantly!

FOREWORD

Mary's *Magnificat*, A Perfect Model of Faith Expression could not have been proposed to us at a more opportune time. On the one hand, it coincides with and contributes to the deepening of our Christian experience during the Year of Faith. On the other hand, it refocuses our attention on Mary as a timeless model for every Christian.

While many aspects on the teachings and questions on Mary lay open for consideration, Father Aaron has chosen in this work the *Magnificat* as the point of departure to speak of Mary's faith. And by working his way patiently through the text, his great contribution has emerged as to how this Lucan song becomes the window through which other texts dealing with Mary's faith can be understood. The importance of the *Magnificat* itself within the Christian Tradition cannot be over-emphasized, a fact that is underlined by its being sung every evening in the liturgy of the hours. Its proposal as a focal point for our reflection on Mary's faith is therefore most appropriate.

I would like to sum up the value of his work in three points. Firstly, it is pedagogic. The author indicates to us how from the ashes of his own struggle to understand Mary, he has searched the scriptures and come to a deeper understanding of the Woman whom Jesus gave to us on the cross as our Mother. This evidence in itself makes Mary a model of faith, namely faith seeking understanding. It suggests to those of us who might be entertaining any doubts about our faith to make recourse to the Word of God for our Lord assures us that "... for everyone who searches finds..." (Matt.7.8).

Secondly, this work proposes a model. By picking Mary and proposing her faith as a model,Father Aaron follows a biblical principle which is beautifully captured in the saying of St. Paul: "Be imitators of me, as I am of Christ" (see 1 Cor. 11.1). Every Christian needs a model. Just as Paul sets himself as a model for his fellow Christians, Father Aaron proposes no less a model for us than the Mother of God – Theotokos. We are invited to re-examine who our real models should be, at a time when so many "mentors" and "idols" are being proposed through the Mass Media. Indeed, we do need a model: Mary makes the perfect one!

Finally, this work is vastly instructive. While scouring a wealth of biblical texts and contemporary authors, the author helps us to resolve a number of sticky points regarding both the *Magnificat* and the teaching about Mary. But he is not content to provide us with information. He challenges us and then motivates us to see how Mary's faith in the midst of adversity could assist us in our own struggles and the value of the salvation that such perseverance in faith would bring us.

While congratulating the author for offering us these rich reflections, it is my prayer that as you read this book, your faith, modeled on the faith of Mary our mother, may blossom into perfection.

Rev. Fr. Michael Kodzo Mensah Rome, August 2013

INTRODUCTION

There are certain things in life which are too beautiful to be forgotten, one of such things is the love of a mother. But the greatest blessing which ever came to this earth was the visitation of the Son of God in the form and habit of man. His life above all lives is, too beautiful to be forgotten; hence we treasure the divinity of His words in Sacred Scripture and the charity of His deeds in our daily actions. This is the man Mary bore in her womb; this is the man Mary celebrates in the *Magnificat*. In the *Magnificat* Mary recognises God's passive gift to her. In other words, she recognises and appreciates God's magnanimous gift she did nothing to merit.

I wish to hold your hands and journey with you into one of the beautiful prayers of our Church, namely the *Magnificat*. It is one of the prayers of the Church that have continued and continue to be prayed so often that it has become a recitation and for that matter it is not really appreciated by some of those who pray them. I think, a reflection would aid us to rediscover the richness of this prayer, and like Mary, we would always sing the praises of God who has called us out of darkness into his wonderful light. Much of what I have written is from my personal reflections over a period of years. I have grown to appreciate Mary personally after a considerable period of time guided by the sound teachings of the Church on Mary. During my childhood days as a Mass Server at St. Anne, Teshie, I observed parishioners gather in a classroom every Saturday, after morning Mass to pray the Rosary. I had never understood why they would separate themselves from the rest of the community to pray since prayer as we all know is a good thing. But to pray in seclusion, for me as a growing child was mind troubling. Even, some visitors to the Parish saw them as a cultic group.

Surprisingly enough, during my studies in the University of Cape Coast, I encountered a similar group in the Catholic Chaplaincy that met also in seclusion Sundays at 3p.m. They invited me severally to their meetings and I always gave excuses. These were moments that offered me the opportunity of knowing them and what they did in seclusion.

In my final year, I served as President of PAX ROMANA and on my visit to a member on admission at the University Hospital, I met a group that called themselves Legionaries. Apparently, they were paying their regular visit to the sick to pray for them in fulfilment of their responsibility as Legionaries. Upon, further inquiry, I was greatly astonished to learn that the secluded group was the Legion of Mary and my heart was troubled. All this while, I was wrong as regards my perception about them. I have always had a soft spot for the vulnerable and after the encounter, I begun to realise that this is a group that can help develop this gift. Soon after entering the Seminary, I enrolled as a member.

I started praying the rosary on my own, and as I reflected on the Mysteries, I noticed that the Legion of Mary held no attraction or interest for many, especially the young people, yet, that is where the treasures hidden in the Church are revealed. In principle, I am, therefore, convinced that every baptised Catholic is automatically a Legionary. You may not necessarily join a Praesidium, but remember that you are a Legionary.

My real motivation for writing this book came when at a Charismatic prayer meeting, I was asked to speak on "Praise and Worship". As I was reflecting on what to tell them, the *Magnificat* came to mind. I did a wonderful presentation according to the estimation of my friends, and that became my source of motivation to develop it further.

In my theological studies in St. Peter's Regional Seminary, I had the chance to visit the Blessed Sacrament every morning, and in that silence, I wrote most of my reflections. It is my ardent prayer and hope that all who read this, will learn to show gratitude to God at all times. Upon the Maternal intercession of Mary, our Mother and Queen, I implore unto you God's manifold blessings.

CHAPTER ONE

A SOUL INSPIRING SONG
(The *Magnificat* Explained)

The Gospel according to Luke is the most comprehensive of the four Gospels and reports several unique accounts that are missing in the other Gospels. Among these unique accounts found in Luke are the most detailed narratives concerning the Annunciation and birth of John the Baptist, the Annunciation and birth of Jesus Christ and the account of the His circumcision, presentation and finding in the Temple. Also, among the accounts unique to Luke are the three canticles or songs of Mary, of Zechariah, and of Simeon. We usually refer to these canticles by their Latin liturgical names: the Magnificat; the Benedictus; the Nunc Dimittis. A canticle (from the Latin canticulum, song) is a hymn or song of praise taken from biblical texts other than the Psalms.

From the New Testament, the Breviary takes the following:

- At Lauds, the "Canticle of Zachary" (Luke 1:68-79), commonly referred to as the "Benedictus" (from its first word);
- At Vespers, the "Canticle of the Blessed Mary Virgin" (Luke 1:46-55),

14

commonly known as the *Magnificat* (from its first word).

- At Compline, the "Canticle of Simeon" (Luke 2:29-32), commonly referred to as the "Nuncdimittis" (from the opening words).

These three canticles are sometimes referred to as the "evangelical canticles", as they are taken from the Gospel according to St. Luke.

The *Magnificat* [Latin: it magnifies], also called the Canticle of Mary, is recorded in the Gospel according to Luke (1:46-55). Because the first word of this hymn is 'magnify', this has always been known as the *Magnificat*. In Greek the word is *megalunei*, meaning ' to make great', 'to magnify.' It is the Virgin Mary's joyous prayer inspired by the Holy Spirit in response to her cousin Elizabeth's greeting (Luke 1: 41-45). This great hymn forms part of the Church's prayer in the Divine Office (Liturgy of the Hours). The *Magnificat* is also a canticle frequently sung (or said) liturgically in Christian church services. In the narrative, after Mary greeting Elizabeth had an extraordinary manifestation. Thus, the child in her womb (John the Baptist) leapt (for joy), the child moves within Elizabeth's womb. When Elizabeth praises Mary for her faith, Mary sings the *Magnificat* in response.

According to Father Oscar LukeFahr, C.M., "This canticle is woven from many Old Testament passages and it highlights a number of themes significant in Luke's Gospel. Among these are Joy,

God's care for the poor and the Lord's faithfulness in fulfilling Old Testament promises" (A Catholic guide to Mary: Christ's Mother & Ours, P. 28).

The Catechism of the Catholic Church describes the *Magnificat* as "the song both of the Mother of God and of the Church" [CCC 2619], and explains this prayer's significance:

Mary's prayer is revealed to us at the dawning of the fullness of time. Before the Incarnation of the Son of God, and before the outpouring of the Holy Spirit, her prayer cooperates in a unique way with the Father's plan of loving kindness: at the Annunciation, for Christ's conception, at Pentecost, for the formation of the Church, His Body. In the faith of His humble handmaid, the Gift of God found the acceptance He had awaited from the beginning of time. She whom the Almighty

made "full of grace"
responds by offering
her whole being:
"Behold I am the
handmaid of the Lord;
let it be [done] to me
according to Thy
word". "Fiat": this is
Christian prayer: to be
wholly God's because
He is wholly ours.
[CCC2617]

--- (Women for Faith & Family – www.wf-f. org August, 2004.).In the *Magnificat*, Mary acknowledges the faithfulness of God which are new every morning (Lam. 3:22-23).

Mary and Elizabeth are wonderful heroines in Luke's account. He loves the faith of these women. The thing that impresses him most, it appears, and the thing he wants to impress on Theophilus, his noble reader, is the lowliness and cheerful humility of Elizabeth and Mary. Elizabeth says (1:43): "And why is this granted to me that the mother of my Lord would come to me?"And Mary says (1:48): The Lord has regarded the low estate of His handmaid." The only people whose soul can truly magnify the Lord are people like Elizabeth and Mary - people who acknowledge their lowly estate and are overwhelmed by the condescension of the magnificent God.

The canticle echoes several Old Testament biblical passages, but the most pronounced allusions are to the Song of Hannah from the Book of Samuel (1Samuel 2:1-10). I think we should notice one other way that Mary's holiness shows itself. Do you remember the story of Samuel and his mother Hannah? Hannah had no children and was taunted by other women because of it and she prayed earnestly that the Lord would give her a son. And he did. Well in 1 Samuel 2 Hannah sings a song of praise which is very similar to Mary's:

Hannah prayed and said, 'My heart exults in the Lord; my strength is exalted in my God. My mouth derides my enemies, because I rejoice in my victory. There is no Holy One like the Lord; no one besides you; There is no rock like our God. Talk no more so very proudly; let not arrogance come from your mouth; For the Lord is a God of knowledge, and by Him actions are weighed. The bows of the mighty are broken, but the feeble gird on strength. Those who were full have hired themselves out for bread, but those who were hungry are fat with spoil. The barren has borne seven, but she who has many children is forlorn. The Lord kills and brings life; He brings down to Sheol and raises up. The Lord makes poor and makes rich; He brings low, He also exalts. He raises up the poor from the dust; He lifts the needy from the ash heap, To make them sit with princes and inherit a seat of honor. For the pillars of the earth are the Lord's, and on them He has set the world. He will guard the feet of His faithful ones; but the wicked shall be cut off in Darkness; For not by might does one prevail. The Lord! His adversaries shall be shattered; Most High

will thunder in heaven.
The Lord will judge the
ends of the earth; He
will give strength to
His king, and Exalt the
power of His anointed.

The parallel expressions, for example, are as follows:

Hannah (1 Samuel 2)	Mary (Luke 1)
v.1 My heart exalts in the Lord...	I rejoice in Thy salvation v.46f
v.2 My soul magnifies the Lord;	
	My spirit rejoices in God my Saviour.
v.49 There is none holy like the Lord.	Holy is His name.
v.4 The bows of the mighty are broken but the feeble gird on strength.	v.52 He has put down the mighty from their thrones, and exalted those of low degree
v.5 Those who were full have hired themselves out for bread, but those who were hungry have ceased to hunger.	v.53 He has filled the hungry with good things, and the rich He has sent away empty.

The parallels are not word for word, neither Mary nor Luke is quoting the Old Testament. Instead it seems to me that Mary was so steeped in Scripture that when she broke out in praise the words that came naturally to her lips were the words of Scripture. Being a young woman, she probably loved the stories of the Old Testament women of faith like Sarah, Deborah, Hannah, Ruth, and Abigail. What an admonition to us all, both women and men, young and old- Mary probably was not more than 15. Let us steep our minds and hearts in the Scriptures day and night so that the words and thoughts of Scripture fill our mouths as naturally as they did Mary's.

How does a soul magnify God? A mouth magnifies God by saying "God is magnificent," by speaking His praises. But no one hears a soul. No one but you and God. But I doubt that Mary was only verbalising a silent prayer. I think she meant that at that moment her soul felt the greatness and holiness and mercy of God. This feeling is primarily one of joy. "My spirit rejoices in God!" Psalm 69:30 affirms this fact when it says, "I will magnify God with thanksgiving." Now we learn the truth that we also magnify God by rejoicing in Him. It is good news to learn that we magnify God by rejoicing in Him. It is good news because we are commanded to glorify or magnify God *(1 Cor. 10:33; Rom. 1:20ff)* and this command could be a terrible burden if we were not told that the only way to fulfill it is to relax and be happy in the mercy of God. That is what magnifies God most.

Like all other New Testament texts the *Magnificat* was originally written in Greek. However, in the Western Church, it is most often to be found in Latin or the vernacular.

In order to properly understand this sacred hymn of praise, we need to bear in mind that the Most Blessed Virgin Mary is speaking out of her own experience, in which she was enlightened and instructed by the Holy Spirit.

For no one can rightly understand God or His Word without such understanding directly from the Holy Spirit. But no one can receive it from the Holy Spirit without experiencing, proving and feeling it. In such experience, the Holy Spirit instructs us as in His own school, outside of which *nothing* is learned *except* empty words and idle fables. When the Holy Virgin, experienced what great things God wrought in her, notwithstanding she was so poor, meek, despised, and of low degree, the Holy Spirit taught her this precious knowledge and wisdom, that God is the Lord whose work consists in this — **to exalt them of low degree, to put down the mighty from their seats, in short, to break whatever is whole and make whole whatever is broken.**

For even as God in the beginning of creation made the world out of nothing even though He is called the Creator and the Almighty, so His manner of working continues still the same. Even now and until the end of the world, all His works are such that out of that which is nothing, worthless, despised, wretched and dead, He makes that which is something, precious, honorable, blessed and living. Again, whatever is something, precious, honourable, blessed and living, He makes to be nothing, worthless, despised, wretched and dying. After this manner, no creature can work; none can produce anything out of nothing.

Therefore, His eyes looks only into the depths, not unto the heights as it is said in Daniel 3:55, "Thou sits upon the cherubim, and beholds the depths"; in Psalm 138:6, "The Lord is the most high, and looked down on the lowly and the high he knows from afar "; and in Psalm 113:5, "Who is as the Lord our God, who dwelled on high, and looked down on the low things in heaven and earth?" For since He is the Most High, and there is none above Him, He cannot look above Himself; nor yet to either side, for there is none like unto Him. He must necessarily, therefore, look within Him and beneath Him; and the farther one is beneath Him, the better does He see him.

However, the eyes of the world and of men, on the contrary, look only above them and are lifted up with pride, as it is said in the book of Proverbs, "There is a generation, whose eyes are lofty, and their eyelids lifted up on high." This we experience every day. Every one strives after that which is above him, after honour, power, wealth, knowledge, a life of ease, and whatever is lofty and great. Where such folks are, there are many hangers-on, all the world gathers round them, gladly yields them service, and be by their side and share in their high estate. Wherefore the Scriptures not vainly describe but few kings and rulers who were godly men. On the other hand, no one is willing to look into the depths with their poverty, disgrace, squalor, misery and anguish. From these all turn away their eyes. Where there are such folk, everyone takes to his heels, forsakes and shuns and leaves them to themselves; no one dreams of helping them or of making something out of them. And so they must necessarily remain in the depths and in their low and despised estate. There is among men no creator who would make something out of nothing, although that is what St. Paul teaches in Romans 12:6, when he says, "Dear brethren, set not your mind on high things, but go along with the lowly." (Piper John, Meditation on the *Magnificat*, Wikipedia, Free Encyclopedia, 1980.)

The First Sorrow of Mary

The Prophesy of Simeon (Luke 2:22-35)

CHAPTER TWO

THE JOY OF MOTHERHOOD
(Background to the *Magnificat*)

When the angel Gabriel *(Luke 1:26)* told the young virgin Mary that she was going to have a child who would be the Son of God and reign over the house of Jacob forever *(Luke1:32ff)*, she said, "How can this be?" He answered her that the Holy Spirit would come upon her for the child's conception would be divine. And then he gave Mary the added confirmation that nothing is impossible with God by telling her that her kinswoman Elizabeth who was old and barren was also pregnant. So according to *Luke 1:39* and following:

> *Mary rose and went with haste into the hill country, to a city of Judah, and she entered the house of Zechariah and greeted Elizabeth. And when Elizabeth heard the greeting of Mary, the babe (that's little John the Baptist) leaped in her womb; and Elizabeth was filled with the Holy*

Spirit and she exclaimed with a loud cry, Blessed are you among women and blessed is the fruit of your womb! And why is this granted to me that the mother of my Lord should come to me? For behold, when the voice of your greeting come to my ears, the babe in my womb leaped for joy. And blessed is she who believed that there would be a fulfillment of what was spoken to her from the Lord!

In his sermon in the Office of Readings on the Memorial of Our Lady of Mount Carmel, Pope St. Leo the Great stated without mincing words that:

A royal virgin of the race of David is chosen to bear the holy child, the divine and human son whom she conceived in her soul before she conceived him in her body. And lest she might be afraid

when something so
unexpected came to
pass, not knowing the
divine plan, she was
shown in her
conversation with the
angel that what was to
be accomplished in her
would be the work of
the Holy Spirit; she will
soon be the Mother of
God without the loss of
virginity. For why
should she lack hope
because of the utter
novelty of such a
conception, when it
was promised that it
would be brought
about by the power of
the Most High. Her
trusting faith was
confirmed by a miracle
already accomplished.
Elizabeth was given
unhoped-for fertility,
so that there would be
no doubt that he who
granted conception to
the sterile could grant
it also to a virgin.

The angel had told Zechariah in **Luke 1:15** that John the Baptist would be filled with the Spirit even from his mother's womb. That is, the Spirit of God would exercise a unique control on this man from the time he is in his mother's womb until he completes his ministry as a grown man. Then Luke gives evidence of this: Mary approaches carrying the Son of God in her womb and little John gives Elizabeth a good kick in the diaphragm. Then Luke says that Elizabeth is filled with the Holy Spirit and cries out: "Mary, my child is leaping for joy. The Holy Spirit has helped him before he can even speak to bear witness to the Lord in your womb" (Emphasis mine). That is all the confirmation Mary needs. She sees clearly a most remarkable thing about God: He is about to change the course of all human history; the most important three decades in all of time are about to begin. And where is God? Occupying Himself with two obscure, humble women-one old and barren, one young and virginal. And Mary is so moved by this vision of God, the lover of the lowly, that she breaks out in song--a song that has come to be known as the *Magnificat*. Having received the Good news about the birth of a son through the power of the Holy Spirit, and having received a confirmation of the conception of John the Baptist by Elizabeth (her cousin) in her old age, Mary, in her confusion set out to render service to her cousin Elizabeth. I am sure that Mary was wondering how she would unravel the uncertainties of her pregnancy to Elizabeth."...

Elizabeth, in some mysterious way, knew that Mary was bearing within her the Messiah. She asked":

Who am l, that the mother of my Lord should visit me? *(Luke 1:43)*

This salutation came from the mother of the King whose path the herald was destined to prepare. John the Baptist still cloistered in his mother's womb, on his mother's testimony leaped with joy at the mother who brought the Christ to her home. Mary's response to this salutation is called the *Magnificat,* a song of joy celebrating what God has done for her. She looked back over history, back to Abraham; she saw the activity of God preparing for this moment from generation to generation; she looked also into an indefinite future when all peoples and all generations would call her "Blessed." Israel's Messiah was on His way, and God was about to manifest Himself on earth and in the flesh. She even prophesied the qualities of the Son who was to be born of her as full of justice and mercy. Her poem ends by acclaiming the revolution He will inaugurate with the unseating of the mighty and the exaltation of the humble. Thus in the midst of this confusion, Elizabeth exclaims immediately she saw Mary: "Blessed are you among women and blessed is the fruit of your womb. And why has this happened that the mother of my Lord should come to me..." (Luke 1:47). Remember that Elizabeth was filled with the power of the Holy Spirit and so immediately she received Mary's greetings she

30

exclaimed: "Blessed is she who believed that there will be a fulfillment of what was spoken by the lord..."Mary knew at once that her undivulged secret has been revealed to Elizabeth. Mary's joy was complete. Mary, apart from visiting her cousin to lend her support saw in Elizabeth someone she could trust. Thus, Elizabeth's exclamation was perhaps a confirmation of Mary's acceptance of the Good news: the Good news about the birth of Christ.

The visitation of Mary to Elizabeth is clouded with **intense joy (Greek Agalliasis)**. Joy, according to Warren W. Wiersbe, is the major theme in Mary' visitation to Elizabeth as you see three persons rejoicing in the Lord namely Elizabeth, Mary and John.

a. **The Joy of Elizabeth** *(Luke 1:39-45)* - Joy is the most infallible sign of God's presence.

Joy is what attracts most people to Church. It is an interior peace that shows itself externally. If we are not joyful, we make the Good news a lie. No one can be joyful without being humble. Joy comes from many sources namely the conviction:

- that God loves me
- that God loves me unconditionally
- that the constant awareness that the Trinity is in me
- that a hope is divine providence

It is a virtue, a gift from God and that we can approach God for mercy and pardon every moment of our lives.

As Mary entered the house, Elizabeth heard her greetings; she was filled with the Holy Spirit. The word that filled her lips was "Blessed." Note that she did not say that Mary was blessed above women but among women, and certainly this is true. While we do not want to ascribe to Mary that which only belongs to God, neither do we want to minimise her place in the plan of God.

The thing that Elizabeth emphasised was Mary's faith: "Blessed is she that believed" *(Luke 1:45)*. We are saved "by grace... through faith" *(Ephesians 2:8- 9)*. Because Mary believed the Word of God, she experienced the power of God.

b. **The Joy of Mary** which culminates in the singing of the *Magnificat*.

c. **The Joy of the unborn son, John** (vv.41, 44). This was probably the time when he was filled with the Spirit as the angel had promised *(Luke 1:15)*. Even before his birth, John rejoiced in Jesus Christ, just as he did during his earthly ministry *(John3:29-30)*. As John the Baptist, he would have the great privilege of introducing the Messiah to the Jewish nation.

Concurrently, Joseph the husband of Mary was in his confused state. **What would any man have done in such a situation?** We are told that Joseph was an honourable man and so did not want to disgrace Mary publicly (lesson for men). In his confusion, the Angel of the Lord appeared to him to give him assurance. The foundation of our encounter with Jesus is the desire for holiness. Joseph we are told, was a holy man and so he took his encounter with the angel with all seriousness and trusted in God's providence. **What about St. Anne and St. Joachim, Mary's parents? How did they receive the news of Mary's pregnancy taking cognisance of her betrothal to Joseph? What were they going to tell Joseph, their respective families and friends?** What an embarrassing situation perhaps, they thought. But since God's gifts and calling are irrevocable, he found solution to this enigma by way of revealing himself to Joseph and assuring him of Mary's situation. Thus in the midst of his troubled state, Joseph waited on the Lord. What a lesson for us! How often have we not been impatient with God and with one another when we encounter difficulties? **How often have we not "cursed" God and one another and as a result of that failed to listen to the solution to our problems?** "They that wait upon the Lord shall renew their strength..." (Isaiah 40:30). Indeed, Joseph waited upon the Lord and he experienced a renewed confidence and faith in God.

CHAPTER THREE

ASSENT OF FAITH
(What made Mary give her fiat (her yes)?)

Tradition has it that the parents of Mary, Anne and Joachim, were in dire need of a child. St. Anne was barren for so many years. But she and her husband waited on the Lord; they trusted in Him and God granted them their request. They asked God for a child, and God gave them not only a child but one special child who became the Mother of God (**Theotokos**). Hence Mary was conceived immaculately. It is highly possible that St. Anne and St. Joachim were not aware of the nobility of Mary and more importantly her Immaculate Conception, but they brought her up in the fear of the Lord. I am sure that they recounted to Mary their own experience of barrenness and how they trusted in the Lord with whom, all things are possible. Mary perhaps imbibed these teachings and when she was confronted with the difficult task of having to choose to be the Mother of our Saviour, even though she did not understand everything, she trusted in God's faithfulness and providence. She may have believed that the God who was faithful to her parents would not forget His handmaid.

Parents and guardians, how are we bringing up our children? What values are we

imparting to them? **What faith- experiences do we share with them such that when they encounter difficulties in their life journeys they can draw lessons from them?** The challenge is ours. **What about us, young men and women, how are we putting into practice these faith-experiences that we hear from Biblical characters, our parents, noble persons of our time?** Mary is an epitome of that faith-experience because shetranslated into concrete response what she learnt from her parents "Behold, l am the handmaid of the Lord, be it done unto me according to thy word."What a faith-proclamation that wrought our salvation. Indeed, Mary deserves to be called blessed and we like Elizabeth who was inspired by the Holy Spirit, would become worthy of divine revelation to also called Mary blessed because she found favour with God whom she trusted.

Elizabeth represents the voice of humanity that sings the blessedness of Mary. This humanity according to Mary's revelation will be the generations to come who will call her blessed. As we can see, Elizabeth foreshadows the prophecy of Mary. She begins the fulfillment of a prophecy yet to be proclaimed in the *Magnificat.*

Mary has found favour with God. Elizabeth calls her blessed. **Why is it difficult for us to call her blessed? Why do we despise her?** We are not doing anything new or strange because whether we acknowledge her blessedness or not, she is blessed. This is the work, not of man, but of the Lord Most High, a marvel in our eyes.

Perhaps another reason why Mary gave her fiat, that which filled the cup to the brim was the fact that she became more convinced when the Angel revealed to her the change in Elizabeth's almost helpless and hopeless condition. Thus, if a woman with more complicated situation of barrenness and menopause is six months pregnant, then it will be far easier in her virginal state, for nothing is impossible with God. I believe strongly that Mary could not initially bring herself to believe that she could conceive without the help of a man until she heard the intervention of God in the life of Elizabeth. This informed her immediate decision to visit Elizabeth thereby calming her suspicion. As a result, Mary joyfully proclaims the *Magnificat.*

The word 'Magnify' connotes enlargement. When Mary says:"My soul magnifies the Lord", she communicates to the world a clear fact that her soul rejoices in the Greatness of God. Her life reflects entirely who God is.

Reading the narrative over again, I find something very much fascinating. It leads me to ask the following basic and fundamental questions: **"Why Mary sung the Magnificat during her visit to Elizabeth and not prior to the visit – soon after the Annunciation?" "was Mary not sure of God's revelation concerning her cousin and needed a confirmation?"** Whenever God calls a person to accomplish a mission, he gives a confirmation or a sign that He is involved and also gives an assurance of His abiding presence. We can only see that through the eyes of faith, which for most people is blinded. Our prayer should be, that beyond the calling to a mission, our eyes be opened "that we may see" the sign of God's involvement with us and His abiding presence.

Joseph Cardinal Ratzinger, in his book, Mary: The Church at the Source, writes something revealing about the Annunciation:

> *He (God) does not simply employ His power to command. In creating man, God has created a free vis-a-vis, and he now needs the freedom of this creature for the realization of his kingdom, which is founded, not on external power, but on freedom (Note St. Bernard of Clairvaux p. 89 of Mary the Church at the source).*

He continues:

> *Without this free consent on Mary's part, God cannot become*

man. To be sure, Mary's Yes is wholly grace. The dogma of Mary's freedom from original sin is at bottom meant solely to show that it is not a human being who sets the redemption in motion by her own power; rather, her Yes is contained wholly within the primacy and priority of divine love, which already embraces her before she is born.

"All is grace." Yet, grace does not cancel freedom; it creates it. The entire mystery of redemption is present in this narrative and becomes concentrated in the figure of the Virgin Mary: "Behold, I am the handmaid of the Lord; let it be to me according to your word(Luke 1:38).(See Hans Urs Von

Balthasar, Joseph
Cardinal Ratzinger,
Mary: The Church at
the Source, P. 89-90).

The *Magnificat* would remain a paradox; an enigma for generations. This is because one cannot fathom how a woman in Mary's situation would sing praises to God. Yet that was what Mary did. The words of the *Magnificat* would reveal later Mary's unshakable trust in God, her humility and above all her service to humanity. No wonder the Church presents her to us as a perfect model of all virtues. The Church celebrates her everyday by praying the rosary in Her honour. Let us recall immediately the words of the Catholic Hymn numbered 288:

Daily, daily sing to
Mary Sing, my soul, her
praises due; All her
feasts, her actions
worship, With the
heart's devotion true.
Lost in wond'ring
contemplation, Be her
majesty confessed: Call
her Mother, call her
Virgin, Happy Mother,
Virgin blest.

Let us look briefly at what she says in her praise of God. I see three distinct sections in the *Magnificat*.

- First, there is Mary's expression of what she feels in her heart (verses 46 and 47), namely joy.
- Second, she mentions what God has done specifically for her as an individual (verses 48 and 49): regarded her lowliness; did great things for her and thus gave her an enduring reputation for blessedness.
- Third, she gives an elaborate description of God in general terms (verses 50-56). This general understanding of the character of God accounts for why He has treated her the way He has in her lowliness, and this leads her to rejoice and magnify the Lord. We will look at these three sections in reverse order.

In the second half of verse 49, Mary makes the general statement that God's name is holy. That is, God's nature, His essence is holiness. He is completely free from sin and His ways are not our ways. He is separate from and exalted above creatures. All His attributes are perfect, and they all cohere in a perfect harmony called holiness. But what Mary stresses is the way this holiness expresses itself. Her words should not be understood to mean that by God's greatness, He is partial to great men, or because He is exalted, He favours what is exalted among men. Just the opposite is the case. God's holiness has expressed itself and will express itself by exalting the lowly and abasing the haughty.

What fills Mary's heart with joy is that God loves to show his favour to the down trodden who calls on His mercy. She mentions this three times: verse 50:" His mercy is for those who fear Him from generation to generation"; verse 52: "He has brought down the powerful from their thrones and lifted up the lowly exalted "; verse 53:" He has filled the hungry with good things." That is one side of God's holiness. The other side is that God opposes and abases the haughty. Mary mentions this three times also: verse 51:" He has shown strength with his arms; he has scattered the proud in the thoughts of their hearts"; verse 52: "He has brought down the powerful from their thrones, and lifted up the lowly"; verse 53: "... sent the rich away empty."

It is clear from Mary's words (and from the different parts of the Bible) that God is not partial to the rich, the powerful or the proud. **How could God be partial to the things which in our world are more often than not substitutes for God rather than pointers to God?** People have perished because they were enamored by pride, power and wealth. So Mary's *Magnificat* is not just recorded out of pure historical interest. There is a word of warning and of salvation here. He is not the least impressed by any of our pride, power or opulence. He has mercy on those who fear Him; those who humble themselves and turn from the ego-boosting accumulation of wealth to the lowliness of self-denial for the sake of others. This is the way God is. This is how His holiness is expressed. Does this not commend itself as true, that the great and holy God should magnify His greatness by blessing the lowly who admire His greatness and by abasing the haughty who resent His greatness?

That is the third section of the *Magnificat*. Now we move back to the second section, verses 48-49a. Here Mary simply sees in her own experience an example of the way God is. He condescends to Mary's lowliness and does a great thing for her: He makes her the "Mother of God!" It is such a singular and unimaginable blessing that all generations from that time on have acknowledged Mary's blessedness. Once Mary learned from the song of Hannah and the Old Testament that God abases the proud but blesses the lowly who look to Him for mercy, now she has found it to be true in her own experience. Probably it is because she had learned it so well from Scripture that she was ready and able to experience it herself.

This is probably the place where our brothers and sisters of other denominations warn against an undue exaltation of Mary as morally unique. Indeed, Mary is unique. No one else bore the Son of God. Our interlocutors say, " The Roman Catholic doctrines of her sinless life, her perpetual virginity, her bodily assumption into heaven have no warrant in the New Testament." In fact, they argued that there is an implicit warning against excessive veneration of Mary in Luke 11:27-28. Luke tells us that once after Jesus had spoken "a woman in the crowd raised her voice and said to him, 'Blessed is the womb that bore you and the breasts that you sucked!' But He said, "Blessed rather are those who hear the Word of God and obey it." At another time (recorded in Luke 8:19-21) "Then his mother and is brothers came to him, but they could not reach him because of the crowd. And he was told, 'Your mother and your brothers are standing outside, wanting to see you.' But He said to them, 'My mother and my brothers are those who hear the Word of God and do it.' They claimed that Jesus was fairly blunt in both of these instances and there surely is no indication that Mary should be venerated in a moral class by herself. If there was anybody who did hear God's word and acted upon it, it was our mother Mary. She said yes to the angel without any hesitation, not even considering what her culture says about what should be done to a girl who gets pregnant at her age, let alone while betrothed to a man. This is the woman the Church presents to us as a model. **How do our interlocutors demarcate between veneration and excessive veneration?**

Let us not just admire her but emulate her example of total faith and trust in God for the righteous shall live by faith. Her spiritual beauty reaches its emotional peak in the first part of her song where she responds from the heart to all God did for her, "My soul magnifies the Lord and my spirit rejoices in God my Saviour."

How does a soul magnify God? A mouth magnifies God by saying, "God is magnificent," by speaking His praises. But no one hears a soul; no one but you and God. But I doubt that Mary was verbalising a silent prayer. I think at this moment her soul feels the greatness and holiness and mercy of God. And the feeling is primarily one of joy. "My spirit rejoices in God!" Psalm 69:30 says, "I will praise the name of God with a song." Now we learn the truth that we also magnify God by rejoicing in Him. And just like Mary did then, I want to close now with this point: it is good news to learn that we magnify God by rejoicing in Him. It is good news because we are commanded to glorify or magnify God (1 Cor. 10:33; Romans 1:20f) and this command could be a burden if we are not told that the only way to fulfill it is to relax and be happy in the mercy of God. That is what magnifies God most.

A cursory look at the words of the Magnificat:

"My soul magnifies the lord, And my spirit rejoices in the lord God my Saviour For he has looked with favour on the lowliness of his servant.

Surely, from now on all generations will call me blessed; For the Mighty One has done great things for me, And holy is his name.

His mercy is for those who fear Him from generation to generation.

He has shown strength with his arm; He scattered the proud in the thoughts of their hearts.

He has brought down the powerful from their thrones and lifted up the lowly; He has filled the hungry with good things and sent the rich away empty.

He has helped his servant Israel, In remembrance of his mercy, According to the promise he made to our ancestors, To

*Abraham and his
descendants forever.*

The chapters that follow will reflect on the verses.

CHAPTER FOUR

WHAT IS YOUR SOUL DOING FOR THE LORD?

(Mary says: "My soul magnifies the Lord, And my spirit rejoices in God my Saviour")
(Luke 1:46-47)

The feeling of the soul and its activities is a mark of high spiritual growth. This is about a spiritual growth only in the Lord from which the soul derives its true and ultimate joy. St. Augustine beautifully puts it: "our hearts (souls) are restless until the find rest in the Lord." We are created to love God and Mary our model shows us this mark. **Have you reached the point where you can feel your soul? Do you realize at any point that your soul is weak or strong?** Most of the time we starve the soul, make it inactive and restless. Mary is the teacher of the soul. The *Magnificat* reveals her role as such as we hear her tell us about the possibility of feeling the soul, its movements, desires and state. This is what Aristotle afirms when he says, "Happiness is the activity of the soul in accord with perfect virtue."

Curtis A. Jahn, in his article Exegesis and Sermon study of Luke 1:46-55 (*Magnificat*) says:

God truly was Mary's
Saviour. Based on

Christ's merits, God saved and redeemed Mary from all sin by not allowing her ever to become sinful. Roman Dogmaticians refer to this as Redemptioanticipata or Praeredemptio (English Preredemption). This Preredemption, according to Catholic teaching, formally constituted in the infusion of sanctifying grace into Mary's soul immediately after its creation.

Again, Spiros Zodhiates, TH. D... In his book: The Song of the Virgin has this to say:

Never did Mary claim to be the Saviour of the world, either before or after the birth of her Son Jesus. In fact, she confessed that she needed a Saviour herself. This is the first statement she made in her hymn of praise to

God...Mary was not dazzled or improperly excited by the prospects of her glorious future. She was not touched by vanity. After her encounter with the angel she said humbly and beautifully, " Behold the handmaid of the Lord; be it done unto me according to thy word" (Luke 1:38). Self had been brought under God's control and God was all to her. The only way to be emptied of self as a goal or supreme value is to be filled with God. That is what happened to Mary. She might naturally have had every reason to feel proud, but she did not. Her only thought on learning of her choice by God to become the mother of His Son was of His greatness and

not her own exalted
position (P.22).

The above is Mary's own testimony of her Immaculate Conception.

The first two lines above of the *Magnificat* reveal the activity of the soul from which happiness is derived. Therefore, true worship and praise of God must come only from the soul (heart) and the spirit and not the body, although it is the temple of the Holy Spirit.

This inspiring song of Mary, expresses beyond imagination, her innermost convictions. Her first impulse, on learning that she was to become the Mother of the Son of God, was to proclaim verbally what was happening in Her soul. By this very act, Mary can be seen as one who understood the words of her Son: "God is spirit and all who worship Him must worship Him in Spirit and Truth."

But the hour is coming
and is now here, when
the true worshippers
will worship the Father
in spirit and in truth.
For the Father seeks
such as these to
worship Him. God is
spirit, and those who
worship Him must
worship in spirit and in
truth (John 4:23-24).

According to St. Bede the Venerable when Mary says this:

Mary is in the first place, acknowledging the special gifts she has been given and then she is speaking of the general blessings with which God never ceases from all eternity to come to men's aid. The soul which magnifies the Lord is the soul of the man who devotes all his spiritual energies to the praise and service of God and by keeping the commandments shows that he keeps steadily before his mind the divine power and majesty.

A man can say that his spirit rejoices in God his Saviour, if he makes it his sole delight to think of his creator, from whom he hopes to receive eternal salvation.

All who have achieved perfection would be justified in using these words, but it was especially fitting that they should be spoken by the Blessed Mother of God, for the privileges accorded her special merits filled her with a great spiritual love for the one she was so happy to conceive.

She had every right to rejoice in Jesus that is in her Saviour, with greater joy than other saints, because she knew that she was going to give birth in the course of time to the one whom she recognised as the eternal author of salvation. For He would truly be her son and her Lord, in one and the same person. As "Mother of God", Mary also acknowledges the fact that Jesus is her God. In the Catholic hymn numbered 108, we sing:

> *O Father fount of joy,*
> *Your glory I adore; O*
> *loving Spirit, praise be*
> *yours, Who gave me*
> *God, my Son!*

The soul (spirit) is a mark of God's ownership on our life (Ephesians 4: 30). It is that which makes us unique that which gives us identity as children of God. I am certain that Mary is only affirming what St. Augustine once said "You created us for Thee and our hearts are restless until they rest in Thee". Indeed if we do not give praise to God, then our hearts will be restless. This is because it is that which gives us identity; identity as children of God.

Again, Mary said that my spirit rejoices in God my saviour. Mary recognizes in her spirit that God is her saviour. Even in her uncertainty, Mary recognizes God as her saviour. Her humility is incomparable, unimaginable, and unfathomable and yet that is what she did. **How many of us, when we are in trouble would not first of all, deny God by feeling ill-treated by Him? How many more would be impatient and seek solution to their problems elsewhere?** Mary in her dilemma praises God and rejoices in Him. She calls God her saviour. **What a perfect model of a woman the Church presents to us?** Mary seems to be saying "Lord to whom shall we go, you have the words of everlasting life". **Shall we emulate her by praising God whenever we are in difficult moments?** The paradox is that when we are in trouble, it is only God who can liberate us. **So why would we do something to further strain our relationship with the only God who can save us?** What a needless pain we bear when we fail to bring to God in prayer all our troubles. Joseph M. Scriven (1820-1886) says it all in his hymn:

> *What a friend we have*
> *in Jesus, All our sins*
> *and griefs to bear,*
> *What a privilege to*
> *carry, Everything to*
> *God in prayer! Oh,*
> *what peace we often*
> *forfeit! Oh, what*
> *needless pain we bear!*
> *All because we do not*

carry, Everything to
God in prayer
(Catholic Hymn Numbered 259).

Warren W. Wiersbe has this to say of Mary's joy:

> *Hers was a joy that*
> *compelled her to lift*
> *her voice in a hymn of*
> *praise. The fullness of*
> *the Spirit should lead*
> *to joyful praise in our*
> *lives (Ephesians 5:18-*
> *20) and so should the*
> *fullness of the Word*
> *(Colossians 3:16-17).*
> *Mary's song contains*
> *quotations from and*
> *references to the Old*
> *Testament Scriptures,*
> *especially the Psalms*
> *and the song of*
> *Hannah (1 Samuel 2:1-*
> *10). Mary kept God's*
> *Word in her heart and*
> *turned it into a song.*

Therefore, in this first part of the *Magnificat*, the focus is on what God did for Mary. Mary acknowledges that God is her saviour. Not only is God her saviour but God has chosen her to be the mother of the Messiah.

The Second Sorrow of Mary

The Flight into Egypt (Matthew 2:13)

CHAPTER FIVE

THE GENERATION THAT WILL CALL MARY BLESSED

(For he has looked with favour on the lowliness
of His servant. Surely, from now on all
generations will call me blessed)
(Luke 1:48)

**My greatest joy is that I will be counted among
the generation that acknowledges Mary as
blessed. What about you?** I once spoke to a
Christian who was having a big problem
accepting Mary and acknowledging Her as
Blessed. I tried to expound the basic teachings
about Mary and Her role in our salvation. But all
she said was: "this woman is a mere instrument
God used to achieve His purpose. She cannot be
my mother and she cannot be blessed." This
sounded pathetic but really unfortunate for her. I
will say that the blessedness of Mary is not
because many Catholics are praying the Rosary
everyday but because God has made Her so. We
only repeat in our own small way what has
already been established by divine initiative.

He had regarded her or been mindful of her
and looked with favour on her are different
renditions of the same idea meaning Mary was in
the Mind of God. She was in the divine plan
specially connected with our Saviour and the

Salvation of Humanity. Many are called but few are chosen. God chose Mary. She did not choose God. And God chose Her for His own purpose. The Lord has indeed showered his graces on her.

Taking a closer look at the verse, we appreciate Mary setting forth the basis for her praise of God. Mary indeed recognises that God looked upon her with favour and affection. Here she describes God's loving care in selecting her to be the Mother of the Messiah.

Also, Mary speaks of herself as the Lord's servant, which expresses a position of subordination and absolute submission to God. She also speaks of her humble, lowly state. Humility here does not mean virtue as Catholic exegetes have long maintained, as if God chose Mary because she had earned God's favour by being so filled with humility. Rather, with this term, Mary is referring to her lowly social status. She was a poor peasant girl; there was nothing notable or great about her as the world views such things. One anonymous author catches the spirit and significance of Mary's words with this paraphrase:

God has regarded me,
a poor, despised and
lowly maiden though
he might have found a
rich, renowned, noble
and mighty queen, the
daughter of princes

and great Lords. He might have found the daughter of Annas or of Caiaphas who held the highest position in the land. But he let his pure and gracious eyes light on one and used so poor and despised a maiden in order that no one might glory in His presence as though he were worthy of this and that I must acknowledge it all to be pure grace and good news and not at all any merit or worthiness.

He goes on to say:

Hence, she does not glory in her worthiness nor yet in her unworthiness, but solely in the divine regard, which is so exceedingly good and gracious that He deigned to look upon such a lowly maiden, and to look upon her in so glorious and honourable a fashion. Therefore, Mary neither gloried in her humility nor her virginity, but only in the gracious regard of God. Hence the stress lies not on the word 'low estate' but on the word 'regarded.' For not her humility, but God's regard is to be praised. When a prince takes a poor beggar by hand, it is not the beggar's low lowliness but the prince's grace and goodness that is to be commended.

Mary recognises that God has given her a special role in his plan of salvation by choosing her to bear the Messiah. Thus because of this special favour shown to her, all generations will call her blessed. This same pronouncement of Mary as blessed and favoured by God occurs every time this chapter of Luke's Gospel is read and heard and every time Christians speak the words of the Apostles' and Nicene Creed and confess that Christ was born of the Virgin Mary. To the end of time, believers will continue to acknowledge the special blessing the Lord gave to Mary.

Having sung the praises of God, Mary acknowledges her humble beginnings even though she is the Mother of God. She never forgot her past or background. How many of us when God has blessed us remember our humble beginnings. Even when she recognises her superior gifts, she recognises that they are gifts: "All generations will call me blessed" (Luke 1:48)." For her part, Mary's own soul "magnifies" not herself but the Lord (Luke 1:46). We forget, but Mary did not forget. She sought everlasting fame, not a fame which is ephemeral. In her *Magnificat*, Mary sees beyond the physical; she sees beyond the present; "henceforth all ages shall call me blessed because the Almighty has done great things for me." Mary could not compare the present suffering to the glory that is to be revealed in her life. Her exultation was in what God is preparing her for, not considering what society will say about her. Friends, God is not interested in our accomplishments, in our successes or failures, wealth, fame but how available we are to Him. Mary is an epitome of that availability. By her faith, she readily accepted the challenge to be the mother of God - a challenge which is a sign of contradiction to many in the world.

For Mary, blessedness means doing the will of the Father. Again she is an epitome of the beatitudes (Matthew 5:3-12).

a. **Blessed are the poor in spirit, for theirs is the kingdom of heaven.** Indeed, Mary is poor in spirit. Hers is the Kingdom of God. This is because she abandoned herself unto her maker- "behold I am the handmaid of the Lord; let it be done to me according to your word."

b. **Blessed are those who mourn, for they will be comforted.** Indeed, Mary went through mournful periods for her son. The prophecy that Simeon made concerning the future of Jesus Christ and Mary's own suffering leaves much to be desired. "A sword shall pierce your own soul and the thoughts of many shall be laid bare". In spite of all these challenging moments, Mary was rewarded and comforted with the assumption and ultimately her coronation as queen of heaven and earth.

c. **Blessed are the meek, for they will inherit the earth.** Again, Mary is an epitome of meekness. She acknowledged her total dependence on God and asked for His will to be done in her life. She realises that it is only in the will of God that she will find peace, and indeed she found peace. Again, her meekness is found in her service to Elizabeth. Luke 1:39

says she went in haste to the hill country in Judea. Can you imagine the mother of God rendering service to the mother of her son's forerunner? Even Elizabeth could not help but exclaim with a loud voice "Blessed are you among women and blessed is the fruit of your womb. And why has this happened to me, that the mother of my Lord comes to me..." (cfLuke 1:42-44). Mary upturned the order of the day- Kings should be served by their subjects. Instead she demonstrated true meekness, showing to the whole world that her Son was to come to serve and not to be served, and to give His life as a ransom for many. By her service to Elizabeth, Mary set the pace for true Christian leadership- selfless service which is supposed to be imitated by all and sundry. Service to one another is at the heart of our Christian calling and this must go beyond all boundaries.

d. **Blessed are those who hunger and thirst for righteousness, for they will be filled.** Did Mary hunger and thirst for righteousness? What does it mean to hunger and thirst for righteousness? Blessed are they who hunger and thirst for righteousness, for they shall be filled..." Was Mary filled at all? Indeed, Mary hungered and thirsted for righteousness because she sought the ultimate in life; her desire to give her all to God. Like Moses, Mary refused to enjoy the fleeting pleasures of this life and chose to submit to the will of God. Mary's hunger and thirst for righteousness was backed by faith because without faith, it is impossible to please God. For whoever would approach God must believe that He exists and that He rewards those who earnestly seek Him (Hebrews 11:6)

e. **Blessed are the merciful, for they will receive mercy.** Was Mary merciful? The wedding feast at Cana says it all. "When the wine gave out, the mother of Jesus said to Him, they have no wine" (John 2:3).Mary was moved with pity (compassion) for the wedding host and guests. She did this request even at the time that Jesus' hour had not yet come. Indeed, Mary sped up her Son's passion and despite her Son's discouraging answer, she told the servants: "Do whatever He tells you."Today, Mary is still telling us to do whatever her son tells us to do for in doing what Jesus tells us to do we will find peace (John 2:5).

Again, her visit to her cousin Elizabeth was a service out of mercy. She saw an old pregnant woman who needed her help. In Mary's desire to render service to Elizabeth, the Lord showed her mercy by Elizabeth's proclamation: "Who am I that the mother of my Lord should visit me at this time...?" Mary seeing that the Lord had shown her mercy exclaimed "His mercy is from generation to generation on those who fear Him." Mary knew that mercy had been shown her by God since her family did not count at all in Israel. This mercy of God shown to Mary led her to humility. This mercy of God was overwhelming for Mary and having been fascinated by this mercy of God, she was spurred on to greater heights in her walk with God.

f. **Blessed are the pure in heart, for they will see God.** It is only one who is pure in heart who can sing the praises of God, for praise is fitting for loyal hearts (Psalm 33:1). In her *Magnificat*, we see a woman so immaculate, Mary who praises God out of the depth of her heart. She did not only see God but bore Him in her womb (Theotokos). She would later suckle him with her breast, and walk this earth with him until his final consummation. Seeing God also means that she met with God's favour. When we also give our all to God, we will meet with God's favour. Mary's purity in heart was also demonstrated in the numerous answers Jesus gives her and the prophecies made about Jesus by Simeon. It is only a pure heart that can bear all these things. A pure heart always seeks the will of God; a pure heart is patient and above all peaceful. Let us look at the instances of Jesus' answers to his mother.

Parents discover their Son in the Temple

Child, why have you treated us like this? Look, your father and I have been searching for you in great anxiety." He said to them "why were you searching for me? Did you not know that I must be in my father's house?" But they did not understand what he said to them... His mother treasured all

these things in her
heart (Luke 2: 48-51).

The answer of Jesus to his parents was piercing and seemingly insulting. But it takes a mother and a father with a patient heart or a pure heart to understand the will of God. Here Jesus' answer appears to suggest that he has another business than the business of a carpenter's shop. My father has sent me into this world on a supreme business of redemption; to make known his love to humanity.

Christ's self-manifestation at the wedding feast at Cana

When the wine got finished, the mother of Jesus said to him "They have no wine" and Jesus said to her, "Woman, what concern is that to you and to me; my hour has not yet come" (John 2: 3-4). Had she been any other mother, she would have been angry with her Son. It takes a pure heart to recognise that the seemingly negative answer which in the mind of readers Jesus gave to his mother, in fact, was an affirmative answer. And so Mary said to the servants, "Do whatever he tells you" (John 3:5). Even now our mother is telling us to do whatever her Son, Jesus Christ tells us to do. Perhaps we have been calling on him for so long a time, but things seem impossible. You are at the verge of giving up because Jesus seems to tell you that my hour has not yet come. Always remember that in his answer, Mary recognised something positive in it and a miracle happened. We have a mother with a pure heart pleading our cause every day. See in Jesus' answer that which is to change your destiny forever. Jesus, therefore, invites us to be happy not because everything is perfect but because you have decided to see beyond the imperfections.

When Jesus seems to choose others over his mother

Then his mother and his brothers came and standing outside, they sent to him and called him. A crowd was sitting around him and they said to him "Your mother and your brothers are outside asking for you. And he replied "who are my mother, and my brothers?" And looking at those who sat around him, he said "Here are my mother and my brothers! Whoever does the will of God is my brother and sister and mother (Mark 3:31-35).

The above words of Jesus are so profound an answer. It is a statement that only a mother with a pure heart, a mother who knows and accepts the will of God,can embrace. Indeed, if there was ever anybody who generously accepted the will of God, it was Mary. Mary noticed that her Son's mission was a universal one, and not limited by tribe, family or nation. In her yes to the angel, Mary accepted the universality of her mission too. It takes a pure heart to recognise that as Christians, our love for each other must cut across cultural and tribal barriers; that nothing must be an obstacle to fulfilling the mission of Christ. It is a mandate we all have to undertake. That is why Christ will say that anyone who loves mother, father, brothers and sisters and even his own self more than him is not worthy of me. This is a total self-giving to Christ and our mother demonstrated this total self- giving with alacrity (Matthew 10: 37-39).

g. Blessed are the peacemakers, for they will be called children of God Was Mary a peacemaker? The circumstances surrounding her being chosen as the "Mother of God", her visit to her cousin Elizabeth, her census experience, the birth of Jesus in a stable, flight to Egypt, the presentation of the child Jesus in the temple, the finding of the child Jesus in the temple, the prophecy of Simeon, the numerous answers of Jesus to his parents (in the Temple, at the wedding at Cana, preaching activities, when he addressed his listeners as his mother, brothers and sisters, his passion and death, among others), all these events make her a peacemaker. Mary is a child of God and at the same time the Mother of God (Theotokos). This is the paradox of her life. Her life is inseparably linked to that of her Son. In fact, they are distinctly inseparable such that to understand Christ, you must understand Mary. What mother in her right frame of mind, knowing that her Son was innocent, will allow for her Son to be condemned? Won't she organise people to defend and set him free? Yet, Mary, an epitome of peace looked on while her son was treated unjustly. It is only a peaceful heart that understands the mind of God and allows God's will to be done even in the midst of bizarre situations. Mary believed that what her Son was going through was to benefit the entire human race. Her mind was that of her Son. She believed her Son's words that "...all who take the sword will perish by the sword" (Matthew 26:52).This was indeed the umbilical cord that bound a mother to her son such that she could not abandon him when all else did, even his Apostles. The bond was so strong that her encounter with her Son at the foot of the cross says it all. Jesus was placed on her laps. What mother would have such courage to do this? When you are a peacemaker like Mary, even when justice is denied you, you will wait upon the Lord. Indeed, Mary is not only a child of God, but the Mother of God, and that is why her Son would not allow her body to see corruption (Assumption) and she became the Queen of Heaven and Earth. She is indeed an epitome of peace.

h. Blessed are those who are persecuted for righteousness sake, for theirs is the kingdom of God. For it is a credit to you if, being aware of God, you endure pain while suffering unjustly. If you endure when you are beaten for doing wrong, what credit is that? But if you endure when you do right and suffer for it, you have God's approval. For to this you have been called, because Christ also suffered for you, leaving you an example, so that you should follow in his steps (1Peter 2:19-21).

Suffering is part of our Christian calling and even the Mother of God went through suffering. St Peter emphasises the need to be joyful when we suffer on account of Christ. This is the only way we can win God's approval.

Mary was noted as a chaste young woman and betrothed to Joseph another chaste man, yet she was found with child. Had Mary committed an act of infidelity? Could this have been the thought going through the mind of Joseph? For her parents, it was unheard of. Their only daughter, whom they had prayed for during Anne's time of barrenness, is now to be a reproach not only to them but to the entire village in Galilee. For the Jews, it was an abomination to get pregnant before marriage. In all these circumstances, perhaps Mary felt confused. Did Mary understand what was happening to her? Was she aware of her new status? In the midst of all these, Mary did three things during her encounter with the Angel which is didactical.

- With the assurance of the Angel, not to be afraid because she had found favour with the Lord, Mary opened up a dialogue with the Angel.
- This dialogue enabled Mary to ask questions"how can this be, since I am a virgin?"(Luke 1:34) This was a logical question any normal human being will ask because a woman can only become pregnant through sexual intercourse. It was not as if Mary doubted what the Angel said but she wanted to be clear on what the Angel told her.

Mary then responded with the fiat:"Behold, I am the handmaid of the Lord, let it be done unto me according to thy word." Mary recognised that faith defies logic. This understanding of Mary wrought our salvation. At least Mary knew that the shame, the confusion, the persecution she will go through could never be compared with the glory to be revealed in her life later on, namely her Assumption and consequently her Coronation. Indeed the Kingdom of God is her's. When we are threatened with life challenges, do we give in to despair or doubt? Like Mary, we may not understand everything that might be happening to us. It may not be logical as well but it is in such moments that we must trust God more and abandon ourselves totally to him as Mary did. Indeed, faith must take over because Jesus assures us of a safe landing. Mary epitomises all those who in the midst of challenges will seek the will of God.

CHAPTER SIX

HAS GOD DONE GREAT THINGS FOR YOU?

(For the Mighty One has done great things for me
And holy is His name)
(Luke 1:49).

With this *for* clause, Mary states exactly why all generations would call her blessed namely, not because she had done great things for God, but because He had done great things for her. Following the line of thought in the song, this verse also introduces a second reason why Mary is praising and rejoicing in God her Saviour: the Mighty one has acted on her behalf and on behalf of all others who fear (believe in) Him.

Reflecting on " the great things" God does for us takes my mind back to a song we used to sing in the Seminary: " Great things happens when God mixes with us." For most people, whatever they have accomplished is greatly due to their own effort. But for Mary, something great has been done for her by the "Mighty One". She speaks using the perfect tense of the Greek with the nuance of an action done in the past with an enduring effect. Therefore, God continues to do great things for her.

"The Mighty One" is the subject of this verse and indeed, the rest of the *Magnificat*. By referring to God as the "Mighty One", Mary focuses on God's attribute of power and then on that attribute, combined with God's holiness and mercy-all description designed to focus attention on God, not on Mary. The reference to God as the "Mighty One" alludes to his power in creating the child in her womb and giving her the role of serving as his Virgin mother. The great things God promised to do, even though biologically impossible (Luke 1:34), God did. Great things here also means the saving events of Israel in Egypt.

Mary was indeed awed by the incarnation of God in Christ. It was the greatest event in the history of the world since creation... she does not speak of what she did for the world in giving it a savior, but of what the savior did for her. The fact that there is a savior will do you no good unless you receive him as your very own Saviour. And your life will never become what it could become by the grace of God, until you willingly obey His call to let Him

have His way with you
(Spiros Zodhiates, TH.
D, P. 54).

One of the greatest joys of Mary was that in spite of her being " of low estate," God did for her what He did. It was indeed a great, a special, a unique calling- but it was not because of any merit of her own; it was all of grace. God's grace and His love are so plentiful that none need be excluded from the full privileges of blessedness in Him.

Mary recognized not only the greatness and the power of God but also that He had acted in her own individual life. There are two classes of persons who acknowledge God's greatness-those who recognize it impersonally and those who have experienced it in their individual lives. **Can you say with Mary, " God has done great things for me"? That He has done great things for the world there is no doubt, but have you willingly permitted Him to work in your own life as Mary did, so that God may accomplish His particular work in and through you?**

An unbeliever met a Christian on the street and asked, " Where are you going?" " To Church," was the answer. " And what do you when you get there?"

" I worship God." "Oh? Well, tell me, what king of God is He, a great God or a small God?" With great reverence the Christian replied, "God is so great that the heavens and heaven of heavens cannot contain Him, yet He is so small that He lives in my heart." This answer closed the unbeliever's lips. For God to do mighty things for us, we must recognize Him as a father from whom comes every good and perfect gift; someone closer to us yet great that the heavens cannot contain Him and at the same time, He is small that He lives in our hearts. He will enlarge our hearts to love Him if we allow Him.

Mary further describes the "Mighty One" as Holy: "Holy is his name." God's name includes everything he has revealed about Himself in Scripture. This idea of the Holiness of God can be traced right from the Old Testament where Moses had an encounter with God at the burning bush. In the same way, Mary who was experiencing some sort of "burning bush" in her life encounters this same God. I say burning bush because in the case of Moses, the bush was burning yet not consumed and we can see also in Mary, a Virgin becoming a mother and still remains a virgin. We see a sharp difference in both instances: Moses observes the burning bush whereas Mary herself is the bush burning: "How can this be since I am a virgin?" The Holy Spirit will come upon you (fire is biblical symbol for Holy Spirit) and the power of the Most High will overshadow you; therefore, the Child to be born will be holy; he will be calledSon of God (Luke 1:34-35).

Without that revelation, we would not know God at all as holy. Saying that God's name is holy is saying that God's Word is described as being holy. He is completely separate from sin in everything He is and in everything He does. By connecting the two lines of this verse with the conjunction "and", Mary reminds us that in his mighty work of salvation, God shows himself as holy. Sin has no place in, with, around or even close to God. By connecting the two lines of verse with the conjunction "and", Mary reminds us that in His " mighty works" of salvation, God reveals His holiness.

God's holy and mighty work is to redeem us sinners from sin and to separate us from sin and all its unholy consequences. Through the mighty, sanctifying work of His Holy Spirit, God makes his people holy, set apart for himself and for his holy purposes.

To say that God's name is holy is to say that God is essentially holy. A name gives an identity. Identity of a person determines credibility. This leads to absolute faith, confidence and trust. Mary absolutely trusted in God and had faith in what God promised he would do. Do you know the One in whom you have put your trust? This is a challenge model for us.

According to Spiros Zodhiates: That God is holy cannot be discovered by searching. The power of God can be discovered, but the holiness of God must be revealed to man by God and accepted by faith. As you read the words of Mary in the *Magnificat*, you mustalways have in mind what revelations the angel Gabriel made to her in Luke 1:28-37. To a great extentwhat she said about God had previously been revealed to her by the angel.

Let us observe the elementsof God's revelation to her through Gabriel and her subsequent affirmation of them:

- That she was the recipient of God's grace (Gk. Kecharitoomenee). The angel tells her she was the recipient of God's unmerited favour in salvation and sanctification. To know that you are saved is a divine revelation, as Paul says in Romans 8:16, "The Spirit itself beareth witness with our spirit, that we are children of God..." In verse 47, Mary calls the Lord her Saviour.
- That she was going to be overshadowed by the power (Gk. Dunamis) of the highest (v. 35). And then later in her hymn of praise she calls the Lord dunatos meaning "strong, mighty"(v.49).
- And then, immediately after the angel referred to the might of God, he added the same attribute to the Lord Jesus (v.35b) as Mary did in her song (v.49). one must read Luke 1:35 and 49 together to see how similar they are and that the attributes Mary ascribes to the Lord were told her in the first place by an angel. Luke 1:35 says, " The angel said to her, ' the Holy Spirit will come upon you and the power (dunamis) of the Most

78

High will overshadow you; therefore the child to be born will be holy (Gk. Hagion); he will be called Son of God. By this, the angel tells Mary the Lord is "power" and "holy." Now let us observe the words of Mary: " For the Mighty (dunatos) One has done great things for me, and holy (hagion) is his name" (Luke 1:49) (P. 58).

What a revelation Mary received about God that He is full of grace, power, and holiness! She accepted it in her own life and she declared it with her own lips. Our own discovery of the power of God can only create fear, as was so often the case in the Old Testament. But how wonderful when the power of God, which is partly discernible by all men by nature, is hemmed in by God's grace on the one side and by God's holiness on the other. The power of God makes you fear Him and run away from Him. But the grace and holiness of God make you go to Him because He is powerful enough to protect you against all dangers and evils. Thus the same power that repels the unbeliever draws the believer. What a paradox!

What is the practical application of all this to your life and mine? Surely, it is that we ought to speak sparingly of God's distinctive blessings, which tend to make us sound like His favourites. Saint Francis of Assisi, when asked how he could achieve so much, replied, "This may be why the Lord looked down from heaven upon earth and said, **"Where can I find the weakest, the littlest,**

the meanest man on the face of the earth?"
Then He saw me and said, " Now I have found him, and I will work through him. He won't be proud of it. He' will see that I am only using him because of his littleness and insignificance."

Another aspect emerging from the holiness of God's name is that it is not just His name but His thoughts, actions, ways, plans, being, possession and the like are included in this holiness. Think about this! Anything that belongs to God must be holy. " For God did not call us to impurity but in holiness" (1Thess. 4:7). This is not an option! Therefore, " You shall be holy for I the Lord your God am holy!" (Leviticus 19:1).

Whenever God blesses us, it is not for our benefit alone. What we fail to recognize is that God's blessings are seldom bestowed on those who seek them merely that their own desire for perfection and personal enjoyment may be satisfied. He fills your cup and mine not merely to satisfy our own thirst, but that His blessings may overflow through us to others in words of witness and deeds of mercy. It is only by letting the living waters flow out to others that we shall find our own hearts continually refreshed as a by-product, but never as the end result of God's blessing on us.

God's mercy which has
been mine is for others,
too, Mary tells us in
Luke 1:50: "His mercy
is for those who fear

Him from generation
to generation

We see that she attributes nothing to her own merits but speaks of all her greatness as the gift of the one who is power and greatness itself, the one who is constantly making his poor weak followers into characters of great strength. But she is right to add: and "Holy is His name", in order to remind her hearers and in fact to teach all those to whom her words would one day reach, that they must believe in his name and call on it and take refuge in it. For they too can achieve a share in eternal sanctity and true salvation, as St. Paul puts it: "For, everyone who calls on the name of the Lord shall be saved"(Romans 10:13). This is the name of which she said earlier: 'My spirit rejoices in God my saviour.

So it has become an excellent and salutary practice in the Church for everyone to sing this hymn daily in the Office of Evening Prayer. In this way the faithful, being reminded more often of the incarnation of the Lord, are moved to devotion, and also strengthened in virtue by regular thought of his mother's example. It is fitting that this should take place at evening prayer, for at the end of the day our minds are tired and prey todistractions and it is very useful to have a moment of quiet to recollect ourselves and gather our thoughts.

This line of the *Magnificat* is a direct consequence of the preceding sentence "From now on all generations shall call me blessed". **Is**

getting pregnant at a tender age a great thing God has done for Mary for which she praises God's holiness? Even in the midst of this, Mary recognises the hand of God in her life; she recognises the holiness of God. I wish to place this line in context.

With her fullest understanding of God's invitation without confusion, Mary makes an assent of faith. "The Obedience of faith" (Rom.16.26; cf. Rom 1.5; 2Cor. 10.5-6) must be given to God as He reveals himself. By faith man freely commits his entire self to God, making "the full submission of his intellect and will to God who reveals," (see Vat. II, Dei Verbum #5) and willingly assenting to the Revelation given by him. Before this faith can be exercised man must have the grace of God to move and assist him; he must have the interior helps of the Holy Spirit, who moves the heart and converts it to God, who opens the eyes of the mind and "makes it easy for all to accept and believe truth."

She was not confused about the fact that she has conceived by the power of the Holy Spirit although her parents and a few others were in the state of confusion. Joseph, the husband of Mary was disturbed and was contemplating of how not to disgrace Mary publicly. Now Mary goes hurriedly to visit Elizabeth her cousin who was in her sixth month of pregnancy. The angel never instructed Mary to visit Elizabeth and neither are we told that Mary went there to seek clarification. However, we can understand this in the light of the Humility of a virgin who having been raised to the status of "Mother of God" would go miles to serve a cousin. Quite fascinating! In our human thinking, Mary rather should be served but we find her going to serve Elizabeth. A characteristic of the first disciple of Jesus in other words the first Christian: "if anyone among you would be the Master, he must first be a servant."

What a sharp contrast between Mary and Elizabeth and yet the pregnancy of Elizabeth was that which fascinated Mary so much that we are told that she travelled in earnest to verify it for herself what the Angel told her "And now, your relative Elizabeth in her old age has also conceived a son and this is the sixth month for her who was said to be barren. For nothing will be impossible with God"(Luke 1: 36-37). Mary might have gone to render service to her cousin, but l believe strongly that she needed a confirmation of what the Angel had told her. This is what Elizabeth expressed in the following words: "Who am l that the mother of my God should visit me?" Who told Elizabeth that Mary had conceived? God? This indeed is the wonder of God. Even in the midst of these challenging moments, Mary sings the *Magnificat*. She acknowledges the holiness of God and her own nothingness. She recognises that she did not merit this opportunity but the grace of God has been poured into her heart. **How many times have we not ascribed to ourselves our success stories, achievements, progress in work, financial breakthroughs,**

among others? When we become the envy of our neighbors, do we attribute to God our success story; do we express these unmerited achievements by singing God's praises? Mary even in her confusion, when she may have become the taunt of her neighbours attributed to God her new status not considering the fact that she is the "Mother of God". This behaviour of Mary can be expressed in the following song:

> *All that we have and*
> *all that we offer comes*
> *from a heart both*
> *frightened and free*
>
> *Take what we bring*
> *now and give what we*
> *need All done in his*
> *name*
>
> *Some would rely on*
> *their power; others put*
> *their trust in their gold*
>
> *Some have only their*
> *saviour whose*
> *faithfulness never*
> *grows old*

(Glory and praise hymn numbered 10)

Self-knowledge means that you come to appreciate what St. Augustine said "You created us for yourself and our hearts are restless until they rest in the Lord". It is this self-knowledge that brought Mary to acknowledge the holiness of God and her own unworthiness. This makes the words of Mother Theresa of Calcutta true when she says: "It was when I discovered my true self that I found God."Self- knowledge is the first step towards knowing God. Mary found this and that is why she could sing the *Magnificat* even when she did not understand fully what was happening to her.

The Third Sorrow of Mary

The Loss of the Child Jesus in the Temple
(Luke 2:43-45)

CHAPTER SEVEN

AUTOMATIC MERCY
(His mercy is for those who fear Him from
generation to generation)
(Luke 1:50)

Mercy is not automatic for all. It is reserved for those who fear the Lord. **What then is the fear of the Lord?** In this verse of her song, Mary included all of God's people who fear Him from generation to generation. We have all received His mercy and experienced His help. Mary specifically names three of such groups to whom God had been merciful: the helpless (Luke 1:51), **the humble (Luke 1:52) and the hungry (Luke 1:53).**

The common people of that day were almost helpless when it came to justice and civil rights. They were often hungry, downtrodden and discouraged *(Luke 4:16-19)*, and there was no way for them to "fight the System." A secret society of patriotic Jewish extremists called "the Zealots" used violent means to oppose Roman domination but their activities only made matters worse.

Mary saw the Lord turning everything upside down, namely the weak dethrone the mighty, the humble scatter the proud, the nobodies are exalted, the hungry are filled and the rich end up poor. The grace of God works contrary to the thoughts and ways of this world's system.

Indeed, the mercy of God is for those who fear him through all generations. God's favour is for all who fear him. He has no favorites. The fear of God is a reverential fear or an awful fear we experience in His presence. Remember how Peter felt when they made a catch at the Lord's command. He exclaimed that he was not worthy. This fear is not the kind that will keep us away from the Lord or see God as wicked and vengeful. It is fear which comes to us anytime we realize our nothingness before Him and acknowledge His greatness and love.

The Psalmist echoes these beautiful words: "O blessed are those who fear the Lord and walk in His ways!" It is not surprising that "Blessedness" and "Fear of the Lord" are sublime virtues of the Lady who is our Perfect Model. Brought up in the fear God by her parents Joachim and Anne, Mary became worthy to be the Mother of God whom she feared. The fear of God is a deep sense of love that keeps a believer away from the near occasion of sin. We err when we lose this sense of fear. Mary never lost this sense. By her life she teaches all that it is possible.

By this recognition, the doctrine of the *Immaculate Conception* has become more profound and pronounced. Each and every one of us has contracted original sin except the "Mother of God", and what Mary means is that her exemption was due to the mercy of God and that

God was capable of raising men and women of all generations to bestow His favour on them like He did to her (Mary). Indeed, the favour of God which Mary received has been received by all generations irrespective of race, colour, sex, religion, and the like.

"It is mercy I desire not sacrifice" says the Lord. This mercy of God resonates in the events of the birth, deeds, passion, death and resurrection of Jesus Christ.

The words *compassion* and *mercy* are and can be used interchangeably. Compassion is the combination of the two Latin words "cum" meaning "with" and "passio" meaning "feeling or suffering." Put together "cum-passio" would mean "suffer with." What Mary gives the world was mercy. Jesus was one like us in all things but sin. In our suffering, we must be encouraged and strengthened since we have one who feels like we feel and suffers with us. In fact, Jesus dies with us. Now, it is our work to believe in his mercy for us so that he may grant us eternal life. For Mary, nothing was impossible with God. **Do you believe in this promise of God which is meant for you, your children and your children's children?** Possess your possession since the foundation of the world for "Blessed be the God and father of our Lord Jesus Christ, who has blessed us in Christ Jesus with every spiritual blessing in the heavenly places, just us He chose us in Christ before the foundations of the world to be holy and blameless before him in love (Ephesians 1: 3-4).All the Lord needs from you is your availability and the recognition that His mercy extends to all who fear Him. Even now, he can choose somebody from your family or even you to accomplish great things. For the fear of the Lord is the beginning of wisdom, greatness and what have you. What Mary became through her Immaculate Conception, was what God destined all of us to become before the foundations of the world. God's holiness and justice without His mercy would be too terrible to contemplate. God's holiness is purity. Man's condition is sinfulness. Sinful man cannot help being afraid when faced with a holy God. Such a God is inherently intolerant of evil. A holy God and sinful man cannot get along together. Not that this is God's fault. God knows that man is miserable in his sin, and that the main reason for this is not the destructiveness of sin but the separation it brings between man and God.

It was within this context that the annunciation and the Incarnation took place. She became very conscious of what the birth of her Son as the God- Man was about to accomplish for all humanity. Thus, in her song of praise, immediately after speaking of God's power and holiness she refers to His mercy. Christ's coming was to be a demonstration of God's mercy to all mankind. There had been other demonstrations of God's mercy, of course, but this was to be the greatest. Spiros Zodhiates has this to say:

It is mercy that sweetens all the other attributes of God. It was mercy that sounded forth the sweetest note in Mary's hymn of rejoicing. Mercy sets God's power at work to help us. It causes His holiness to find a way of bridging the gulf between Himself and sinful man. That bridge was Christ, who was to be born for the very purpose of dying as the sacrifice that would satisfy God's justice (P. 64-65).

God's mercy is indeed from generation to generation. The Old Testament attests to this fact. For instance, during Moses's encounter with God, he told God, " Show me your glory, I pray." And He said, " I will make all my goodness pass before you and will proclaim before you the name, " The Lord"; and I will be gracious to whom I will be gracious and show mercy on whom I will show mercy" (Exod. 33:18,19). God did not mention "power, holiness, justice," but His mercy. Since Christ's birth was the beginning of the most important demonstration of God's mercy, and since God's glory is predominantly shown in His mercy, this event of the incarnation can be said to be the most glorious one. The incarnation was basic, of course, to the crucifixion and the resurrection, and when Scripture speaks of these events the incarnation must always be included, for it was the necessary prerequisite to them.

Spiros Zodhiates Observes that:

> *Mary recognizes that, in spite of her blessed function of becoming the mother of the incarnate Son of God, she is not to be the dispenser of God's mercy in any way different from that in which all the blessed are called upon to be merciful. "Blessed are the merciful," said Christ, "for they shall obtain mercy" (Matt. 5:7). We must be careful to distinguish between God's mercy and ours. Man is a sinner who must suffer the consequences of his sin. God's mercy cannot be manifested at the*

expense of His justice.
To satisfy His justice
and at the same time
provide forgiveness for
the sinner, He sent His
Son into the world to
be born of a virgin, to
live as the God-Man,
and to die and rise
again. He bore the
penalty for our sin and
therefore it is He who
can exercise this mercy
that brings us eternal
life, salvation, and
forgiveness. No one
else has this privilege
or authority. Neither
Mary nor any angelic
or human being can
show to man the mercy
that brings
salvation(P.65).

When man relies on the mercy of God through faith in Christ, there is a change in his very nature, making him a new creature in Christ (II Cor. 5:17). This is what Mary communicates to us in the verse. When I as a sinner receive this mercy or grace of God, being changed, and becoming a channel of His grace, I also become merciful. But I am not in a position to save others, only to introduce others to Christ the merciful Saviour.

This is exactly how Mary felt when she realized she was going to bring God's Son into the world. She herself was saved by Him and she proclaimed Him to be the Saviour of the world. There is not the faintest suggestion that she considered herself able to save anyone, either herself or others. She, like every other saved child of God, became through Christ a merciful person; but her mercy was expressed in the form of compassion to others, not in delivering them from their state of sinfulness to a state of salvation. It is completely unscriptural to cry to the Virgin Mary to be merciful to you in procuring your salvation. This is the prerogative of the mercy of God the Father, God the Son, and God the Holy Spirit. No one can forgive sin perpetrated against God but God Himself. I can forgive your sins against me only on the human level, never the divine.

Spiros Zodhiates says again:

> *When the angle*
> *Gabriel told Mary that*
> *she was going to be the*
> *recipient of this*
> *original grace or*
> *mercy of God, he said,*
> *"Hail, thou that art*
> *highly favoured, the*
> *Lord is with thee:*
> *blessed art thou*
> *among women" (Luke*
> *1"28). The Greek word*

translated "highly favoured" here is kecharitoomenee, "graced" (from charis, meaning "grace"). Paul uses the same word as he speaks of the believers accepted in Christ in Ephesians 1:5- 7, "Having predestinated us unto the adoption of children by Jesus Christ to himself, according to the good pleasure of his will, to the praise of the glory of his grace, wherein he hath made us accepted [echaritoosen, 'graced'] in the beloved. In whom we have redemption through his blood, the forgiveness of sins, according to the riches of his grace."

In the early Church we fine that great grace was the portion of all who believed. "And the multitude of them that believed were of one heart and of one soul ....and great grace was upon them all" (Acts 4:32,33). Mary received the grace that was bestowed upon her by Him who was "full of grace" to all believers, for "unto every one of us is given grace" (Eph. 4:7). Indeed Paul encourages the Corinthians to aspire to abundant grace. "And God is able to make all grace abound toward you; that ye, always having all sufficiency in all things, may abound to every good work" (II Cor. 9:8).

In this verse also, Mary is quick to add that the beneficiaries of the mercy of God are those who fear Him. This fact is buttressed again by Spiros Zodhiates when he says:

> *The fear of God in man
> has a two-pronged
> direction. It makes you
> know yourself as a
> sinner. It makes you
> turn to God for mercy.
> And, once mercy fills
> your soul, the fear of
> God becomes the
> constant fellowship
> with God, for He abides
> in you and you abide in
> Him. The moment you
> possess the mercy of
> God, which is the
> product of His love for
> you, all morbid fear
> and terror disappears.
> Listen to John: "There
> is no fear in love; but*

*perfect love casteth
our fear: because fear
hath torment. He that
feareth [this is the fear
of being left alone and
desolate without God
in this life] is not made
perfect in love" (I John
4:18).*

No doubt Mary included herself in this great company of people who, fearing God, became the recipients of His grace. Hers was indeed a great privilege to become the mother of the Lord Jesus, but to her it was an even greater privilege to have the fear of God in her heart and thus become the recipient of His mercy. **Does this shock you?** Remember, it is not I who say it but the Lord Jesus Himself. One day as He was teaching a gathering of eager listeners, a dear woman who may well have been aware of the blessing of motherhood said to the Lord, "Blessed is the womb that bare thee." To which the Lord replied, "Yea, rather, blessed are they that hear the word of God, and keep it" (Luke 11:27,28). This is equivalent to fearing God and receiving His mercy. Our Lord was in no way implying by these words that His mother did not satisfy the conditions of true blessedness, because "Mary," we are told, "kept all these things, and pondered them in her heart" (Luke 2:19). What He wanted to stress, however, was that, no matter how great or religious privileges, the fundamental need of the human heart is the mercy of God, the fear of God. **Do you realize that you can be a minister, a priest, a bishop, and yet be devoid of the grace of God?** Your function in the Christian Church is not as important as your personal relationship with Christ. It is this relationship of a redeemed sinner to a holy God alone that makes you blessed.

Let us learn one lesson from all this. All men, irrespective of their status in society, are viewed as equal before God, in that they are sinners who are saved, not by what they accomplish, but by seeking the receiving God's mercy through their fear or reverential awe of the Lord. Mary the mother of Jesus was saved, not because of what she did in bringing the Saviour into the world, but by receiving Him just as everyone else is called upon to receive Him.

Whether or not we understand or like it, we all enter upon life with different capacities for learning and assimilation. But the basic things of life God has made available for the enjoyment of all-air, nature, the sun, water, food. These are the common property of rich and poor, the powerful and weak, the honored and neglected, to a varying degree and according to the ability of each. **But who can say that he is deprived of the elementary need of air?** Similarly the fear and mercy of God are available to all, and in the same manner. There is only one way you can receive the benefits of air, and that is by breathing it into your lungs, no matter how high or how humble you station. And there is only one way you can obtain God's mercy, and that is by appropriating it through faith in Jesus Christ. As Canon Liddon says, "Only one woman could be the Mother of the Most High Holy when He vouchsafed to enter our human world; but there is no reason why each and all of us should not know by experience what the Apostle means by that astonishing yet most blessed saying, "Christ in you, the hope of glory" (Cor. 1:27)." (The *Magnificat*, p. 56.) That's what Mary had. That's what she treasured most – the implication of the presence of Christ, not as mere flesh but as the eternal Word, the Logos, who had always been with the Father, God. Her greatest privilege can be yours, although her function of being the mother of the Lord Jesus could only be hers. But we can all have the same blessedness as she, sharing in her relationship with Christ by our obedience to God's will. Our Lord Himself declares it: "Who is my mother? And who are my brethren? ...Whosoever shall do the will of my Father

The Fourth Sorrow of Mary

Mary meets Jesus on the way to Calvary

The Fifth Sorrow of Mary

Jesus dies on the Cross (John 19:25)

CHAPTER EIGHT

OUR ACTIONS MUST CORRESPOND WITH GOD'S REACTION

(He has shown strength with His arm; He has scattered the proud in the thoughts of their hearts)
(Luke 1:51)

In the Gospel we hear of two scatterings. One in the *Magnificat* and the other in the teachings of Jesus: "He who is with me gathers and He who is not with me scatters." In the first instance the Lord scatters but in the second instance those who scatter are against the Lord. Interesting! The question addressed to the *Magnificat* specifically is: "what is scattered?" "Does the Lord scatter Himself or he uses men?" "Are you scattered or you are scattering?" "What are you scattering?"

This verse states the fulfillment of the Abrahamic covenant; he has completed his plan of salvation for the fallen human race through the coming of His Son. Certainly, part of this plan included such specific historical events as making the family of Abraham, Isaac, and Jacob into a nation. It involved bringing enslaved Israel out of Egypt under Moses and into the Promised Land under Joshua. It included establishing the royal line of David, sending the Prophets, and all God did in the Old Testament so that his covenant with Abraham would be fulfilled. Mary was witnessing the fulfillment of that covenant with the coming of God's Son who would suffer and die, rise again and ascend into Heaven, from where he would send forth his Holy Spirit on his new covenant people.

In bearing the Son of God, Mary was fully aware of the fulfillment of that promise God made to Abraham from generation to generation. Thus, this verse of the *Magnificat* deals with God's providence as it applied to the whole earth in relation to the birth of Christ. That momentous event that occurred in Bethlehem of Judea was destined to shape the course of all history.

The ultimate fulfillment of the covenant will take place when Christ returns on the Last Day to raise the dead and usher in the new heaven and new earth (2 Peter 3:13). I, therefore, understand Mary as speaking here of God's plan as accomplished, in Jesus Christ whom she has conceived in the womb indicating both the present reality and the future reality of Christ 's coming.

Indeed, Mary also recognised that the arm of God was stronger than any human endeavour. When human arm gathers or scatters without God, what is gathered or scattered is vain. It is by the arm of God that the Israelites fled from Egypt. Great things happen only by the strength of His arm. Just think of what you stand losing if you acted independent of God who is able to do immeasurably more than we can even imagine. In this context, Mary acknowledges the fact that the arm of God actually turned 'tables' round in her favour and would do same for anyone who would trust. At the wedding feast in Cana, she encourages the servants to "do whatever he (Jesus) tells you to do."

Reflecting on her own background: coming from a village of Nazareth, not even counted among the tribes of Israel of which Nathaniel says "can anything good come from Nazareth", Mary could not but say that, God has scattered the proud in the thoughts of their hearts. Mary, from the lowly people, whom society rejects, taunts, disregards, God has raised above human understanding. This arm of God was that which moulded and formed man. That same arm led the people of Israel through the Red Sea and this same arm having seen the affliction of fallen man decided to restore him to his lost dignity through a humble servant Mary. This was to fulfill what was spoken in Genesis that "I will put enmity between you and the woman and between your offspring and hers; he will strike your head and you will strike his heel,"

Even right at the conception of Jesus in her womb, Mary recognised that at his birth many kings and powerful rulers would be toppled; many who hear of him will be envious. We can talk about King Herod, Pilate, the Governor and Emperor Caesar and the many who championed the course of his death: the High Priest, Chief Priests to mention but few. More especially even after his death, the mere mention of his name met with persecution, and so the persecution of his followers especially that by Emperor Nero is a case in point.

In fact, Mary understood vividly what Simeon said,"This child is destined for the rising and falling of many in Israel and to be a sign that will be opposed so that the inner thoughts of many will be revealed and a sword will pierce your own soul too"(Luke 2:34-35). Mary experienced persecution herself; she experienced what it means to be in need herself at Bethlehem when she needed a place to deliver her Son.

Indeed, God has brought down the powerful from their thrones and lifted up the lowly. Mary has become a living witness of this fact that she will proclaim this even before the reality of what was promised becomes manifest as the "Mother of God." Mary presents to us an example of someone who will praise and glorify God before something is accomplished in her life.

How many of us will
not wait until good
things come our way
before we praise God?
Let us learn from
Mary.

The Lord demonstrates His strength, His omnipotence, according to a timetable and plan.

His salvation or the dispensing of grace and mercy, as well as, His judgment, is not the result of an arbitrary whim but of a careful strategy of reaction toward our action. To those who fear and reverence Him He extends grace. To those who defy Him He extends judgment. For every action of man there is a divine reaction. This principle was enunciated in Genesis 4:7, when God rejected Cain's offering: " If you do well, will you not be accepted? And if you do not do well, sin is lurking at the door; its desire is for you, but you must master it"

The Sixth Sorrow of Mary

The Piercing of the side of Jesus and
Mary receiving the body of Jesus in her
arms (Matthew 27:57-59)

CHAPTER NINE

GOD BRINGS DOWN, LIFTS UP, FILLS AND SEND AWAY

(He has brought down the powerful from their thrones and lifted up the lowly; He has filled the hungry with good things and sent the rich away empty) (Luke 1: 52-53).

I call this the Four Dimensions. Just try making the sign of the cross and you will be amazed how this comes out clearly. Before making the sign of the cross it must dawn on you that God brings down. A demand for a sober and humble attitude from thence is placed on you. From the Son to the Holy Spirit, God lifts up. He fills with the Holy Spirit and sends away. **Is this not amazing?**

In this section, Mary could not help but think of how God mightily overruled the ungodly rulers of the world at Babel, Egypt, Assyria, Babylon, and Persia during the Old Testament times. The same was true of the Ptolemies and Seleucids during the Intertestamental period. None of the powerful men in those periods could stop the Mighty One from carrying out his saving plan. Even the Roman Caesar and King Herod would have to bow to God's plans, which would be fulfilled. The Virgin had conceived and would bear a Son and call his name Immanuel, and he will reign over the house of Jacob forever. God had kept his promises: he had performed the mighty deed of choosing a lowly peasant girl from out of the way Nazareth to bring his Son into the world. Mary was nothing great in the eyes of the world and she had nothing meritorious to offer God that He should choose her. She was a child of grace, as is the plan for all God's children. Nothing in her hands did she bring; simply she said yes and God did in her this great thing. She clung to her Saviour who was her Son and to his cross. God has raised up with Christ all such people who are humble before him and seated them with Him in the heavenly realms in Christ Jesus *(cf Ephesians 1:3-4, 2:6).* He has exalted them to the status of being God's children," Heirs of God and co-heirs with Christ" *(Romans 8:17).*

Mary describes God's mighty deed of salvation with still another contrast. The hungry and the rich ones are two classes of people but viewed from a different perspective. The two classes still are believers and unbelievers, the penitent and impenitent, the humble and the proud, those who stand before God with empty hands which can only receive from God's bounteous mercy and those who try to come to God their hands filled with the treasures of their own merits by which they think they deserve God's favour. They are the same two kinds of people as the Pharisee and the Tax Collector in Jesus' parable *(Luke 18:9-14).* The tax collector went home filled with good things: God's gift of justification, God's gracious pardon for sin, God's approval, heaven itself. The Pharisee went home empty handed and empty hearted. He had no room for God's love in his heart because his heart was filled with the vanity of self-righteousness and self -love. Indeed, God continues to send away empty, those who are self-righteous, and he fills with good things those who come empty and ready to be filled. St. Paul puts it beautifully when he says:

> *Therefore, since we are justified by faith, we have peace with God through our Lord Jesus Christ, through whom we have obtained access to this grace in which we stand and we boast in our hope of sharing the glory of God. And not only that, we also boast in our sufferings, knowing that suffering produces endurance and endurance produces character and character produces hope and hope does not disappoint us, because God's love has*

been poured into our
hearts through the
Holy Spirit that has
been given to us
(Romans 5:1-5).

God has shown mercy to those who fear him, but he has scattered the proud and arrogant. He has brought down the high and mighty of this world who oppose him, but he has raised to high and status of sonship, those who have been humbled by the law to see that nothing good lives in them by nature and trust rather in Christ and his goodness in salvation. God has filled the desire of those hungry for Christ's saving righteousness while he has sent away empty-handed all those who think they are rich in themselves before God.

This is God's principle of the great reversal, as it has been called. It is the paradoxical great reversal Jesus speaks of in so many of his parables. "Everyone who exalts himself will be humbled and he who humbles himself will be exalted" (Luke 14:11; Matt. 23:12). "There are those who are last who will be first and the first who will be last" (Luke 13:3). See also the Beatitudes in Jesus' Sermon on the mount. The Apostle Paul expounded this same principle of the great reversal in 1 Corinthians 1:18-31:

For the message of the
cross is foolishness to
those who are
perishing, but to us

who are being saved, it
is the power of God.
For it is written: I will
destroy the wisdom of
wise; the intelligence
of the intelligent I will
frustrate." Where is the
wise man? Where is
the scholar? Where is
the Philosopher of this
age? Has not God made
foolish the wisdom of
the world? For since in
the wisdom of God the
world through its
wisdom did not know
him, God was pleased
through the foolishness
of what was preached
to save those who
believe. Jews demand
miraculous signs, and
Greeks look for wisdom
but we preach Christ
crucified: a stumbling
block to Jews and
foolishness to Gentiles,
but to those whom God
has called, both Jews
and Greeks, Christ the
power of God and the
wisdom of God. For the

*foolishness of God is
wiser than man's
wisdom and the
weakness of God is
stronger than man's
strength.*

St. Paul says again:

*Brothers, think of what
you were when you
were called. Not many
of you were wise by
human standards; not
many were influential;
not many were of
noble birth. But God
chose the foolish things
of this world to shame
the wise; God chose the
weak things of this
world to shame the
strong. He chose the
lowly things of this
world and the despised
things and the things
that are not to nullify
the things that are, so
that no one may boast
before God. It is
because of him that
you are in Christ Jesus
who has become for us*

113

wisdom from God- that
is our righteousness,
holiness and
redemption. Therefore,
as it is written: Let him
who boasts, boast in
the Lord. (Emphasis
mine).

God's great reversal takes place through the preaching of law and gospel. The message of the *Magnificat* that scorns and condemns all human pride and self-righteousness is squarely aimed at our sinful hearts and our natural-born ways of thinking and acting. Mary's words accuse and convict us all and it brings us comfort too especially for those whom God knocks down with the law he also lifts up with the gospel. Through Christ, God graciously helped us in every way. With these same thoughts, Mary concludes the *Magnificat* as we will see pretty shortly.

I believe strongly Mary was talking about spiritual feeding and not physical feeding otherwise her statement will be a paradox. The rich do not need to be fed but the poor do. Thus for God to have fed the hungry with good things implies bringing hope into the life of those who are oppressed and poor in the community. Indeed, for her to have come from a family or a tribe which was not regarded in any way; a village of Nazareth of which Nathaniel says **"Can anything good come from Nazareth?"** Mary knew what was at stake. Again, many thought that the coming of the Messiah was to continue the status quo–in that he was going to identify himself with the aristocracy in suppressing the poor, but Jesus caused a scandal when all the Jewish authorities saw was that he was moving with the poor, tax collectors and all those considered sinners among the Jewish people. Jesus displaced the status quo and was calling for the toppling of the unjust structures of the Jewish society. But the Jewish authorities again missed this opportunity because they failed to see through the eyes of the Messiah. Thus the rich He has sent away empty and the poor or the hungry He has filled with good things namely: Zacchaeus, Bartimaeus, the repentant thief on the cross, the daughter of the Syrophoenecian woman, the woman suffering from haemorrhage; indeed, he has come to do same for all who have become wanderers in the house of God. Money cannot buy salvation; it is a free gift from Jesus himself. He has thrown the invitation to us all. Ours is a response in faith. **Are you rich yet hungry?** Come to the source of living water that you have forsaken all these years and he will fill you with good things.

The Seventh Sorrow of Mary

The Body of Jesus is placed in the tomb
(John 19:40-42)

CHAPTER TEN

THE PROMISE OF GOD IS FOR ALL

(He has helped His servant, in remembrance of
His mercy, according to the promise He made to
our ancestors, to Abraham and to His
descendants forever)
(Luke 1:54-55)

Whenever the Bible speaks of God remembering, as Mary says here, it is employing a figure of speech called an anthropopathism, assigning human emotions and mental activities to God. When Mary says God remembered his mercy to Abraham, etc., she means God has done something to fulfill his covenant with Abraham. Mary is referring to the unilateral covenant of salvation the Lord made with Abraham and his seed (Genesis 12:1ff. 22:15ff. etc). Because of the incarnation of the promised seed par excellence, Mary is celebrating the fulfillment of God's covenant promise of mercy. All believers in Christ, the promised seed, count themselves as beneficiaries of this promise of help and mercy to Abraham's spiritual seed (Galatians 3:26, 29), and celebrate this promise in faith as Mary did.

Mary, also, shows that her faith is firmly grounded in the scriptures. Everything Mary knows and says about the Lord namely his mighty deeds, his covenant, his promises of salvation is grounded in scriptures, the inspired written records of what God spoke to her Jewish forebears. Mary's worship and praise of the Lord flows out of her knowledge of the Scriptures and God's plan of salvation recorded in them. Our faith and our worship and the praise of God flows from the same source. In fact, with her entire song, Mary shows herself to be an ideal model for our worship of God today. Her worship focuses on God and his gracious promises, what he has done for us. Her worship centers in Christ as the fulfillment of all God's promises of mercy to sinners. Her worship is based on Scriptures, and flows out of them. And her worship comes from her heart; in repentance and faith she applies law and gospel to herself, resulting in joy-filled praise and wonderment at the mighty and faithful saving mercy of God in Christ.

The Virgin Mary never forgot the fact that she was Jewish. God could have chosen a woman of another nationality to give birth to His Son, but He chose a Hebrew girl. Mary knew that the incarnation of God in Christ was the demonstration of God's mercy- toward her, toward all mankind and toward Israel.

She recognized Israel's distinction from the rest of the world in God's providence and plan. And part of this plan was that the Lord Jesus was born of a Jewish mother. We cannot understand the Scriptures unless we recognize, as did Mary, this special plan and purpose of God for Israel.

Mary was well acquainted with the many interventions of God throughout Israel's long history. **Why should He show them such favour?** She humbly confessed that neither she nor her nation deserved it. **Why should God so constantly intervene on behalf of the Jews, and why these promises to protect them to the very end? Why should He make them the guardian of His revelation and will?** Don't expect anyone fully to know the answer. Mary herself attempted no explanation. She simply stated the fact.

From this we can see that God is sovereign in all that He does. This is not arbitrariness, as some misunderstand it, for God has His reasons, based on His infinite wisdom, which He does not always choose to reveal to us. **We act the same way toward our children, do we not?** We have to make choices with regard to their lives when we deem them incapable of making their own. **When we regulate their diet, their hours of sleep and so on, are we being arbitrary or wise?** Why attribute wisdom to such acts of our own and yet arbitrariness to God's acts towards us His creatures.

St. Paul puts it succinctly, "I will have mercy on whom I will have mercy" (Romans 9:15). In other words, in His all-encompassing wisdom God does whatever He wants to, not only in the area of His power but also of His will. We humans are possessed of a passion for equality, but God does not seem to share in that passion. He does not create all people equal.

We would have the right to question this only if we had the power to be creators ourselves. A creature of so far less power than God cannot possibly claim the right to question the wisdom or the will of an omniscient and omnipotent God. We can observe how God works, but we lack the capacity always to understand why He works the way He does. He does not create all mountains equal, nor all trees equal, nor all men with equal intelligence and abilities. The distribution of His gifts and privileges is never equal. He gives to each as He pleases and as He gives He will judge. He will never ask the person to whom He has given five talents to give an accounting of ten; but He will ask for an accounting for ten from him to whom He gave ten. Insofar, then, as God's choice of Israel to receive His special attention as a nation is concerned, it is in perfect accord with His absolute sovereignty. The reasons lie beyond our understanding; therefore, they should lie beyond our criticism. Let us accept God as He manifests Himself to mankind and instead of rebelling against His decisions let us cooperate with them.

Spiros Zodhiates has this to say about God's promise and mercy towards Israel:

God did not choose
Israel in order to
enslave her. In fact, the

verb translated "Helped" comes from the Greek verb antilambanomai which basically in the New Testament means, " to show serious concern for the weak" (Acts 20:35), " to show divine help." God showed concern for Israel and here as elsewhere He calls him His servant. The word servant is not the Greek word doulos meaning slave, but paidos (the genitive of pais), whose primary meaning is child. The verb indicates rendering help by a superior to an inferior, to a child, to a servant, who stand helpless. We see an indication here that the Lord's attitude of favour to Israel did not have any selfish purpose. It was not so that God might get the most service out of

*Israel, but that He
might show mercy to
them (P.137).*

God in His sovereign acts is never motivated by selfish reasons. Whenever He shows favour to someone, it is not in the expectation of some return, but merely because of the need that the person or group has of Him. God's choice of Israel was neither due to their merit nor to His expectation of anything great from them as far as He was concerned. This is the meaning of Mary's words, " ...in remembrance of His mercy..."

What God did in regard to Israel He did out of mercy, in the same away that he acted in regard to Mary in selecting her to be the mother of His Son and as He does in regard to all humanity. We are recipients of the mercy of God. Mercy is not something that we deserve. Beggars cannot be choosers. Therefore, whether God's mercies towards us are great or small, they should stimulate nothing but thanksgiving. The sending of the Lord Jesus Christ into the world was a demonstration of the exercise of God's memory of His promise of mercy. God remembers what He promises and He never fails to keep His word.

The reason why Mary mentions Israel and Abraham in the *Magnificat* is to show that not only was she chosen in spite of the fact that she did not merit this favour of God (Luke 1:48), but also the fact that she was Jewish was an indication of God mercifulness towards Israel and toward Abraham. Again, this was not because either

Israel or Abraham deserved this special treatment of God.

The Jews were not chosen by God because they were virtuous above all other nations, but simply because He was God and He could exercise His sovereignty. If the rabbis claimed that God chose Abraham because of his obedience, especially as typified in his willingness to sacrifice Isaac (Genesis 22:12, 18; 26:5), Paul replied that Abraham's faith preceded his work, since he would not have obeyed had he not first believed God's promise; and in support of this he quotes Genesis 15:6, " And he believed the Lord and the Lord reckoned it to him as righteousness" (Rom. 4:3, Gal 3:6).

As I conclude my reflection on the *Magnificat*, I wish to state that after enumerating the works of God in her and in all men and women, Mary returns to the beginning and to the chief thing. She concludes the *Magnificat* by mentioning the greatest of all God's works namely the Incarnation of the Son of God. The purpose of the Incarnation is to redeem humanity from the clutches of the devil, sin, death and hell, and to lead them to righteousness, eternal life and salvation. This is the help of which Mary sings and that is the help of which we sing and preach even today.

In this last verse, Mary focuses on what God did for Israel

In this verse, Mary acknowledges the faithfulness of God towards Israel especially as regards the promise God made to Abraham and his descendants. Mary herself is a beneficiary of this promise and could not fathom how a poor village girl like her could become the final bearer of this promise namely Jesus Christ. The long awaited Messiah has come especially when He is least expected. He came when Israel has gone through a long period of suffering due to their unfaithfulness to God. To say the least, he was born into a family that nobody expected. For Mary, this was least expected in her family and it happened. No wonder, Simeon in his Nunc Dimittis says the following:

At last all powerful Master,

You give leave to your servant

To go in peace, according to your promise For my eyes have seen your salvation Which you have prepared for all nations, A light to enlighten the Gentiles

And give glory to Israel your people. (Luke 2:29-32).

Fortunately, we are part of the present generation that has witnessed and continue to witness powerfully the fulfilled promise namely Jesus Christ. He is present to us in the Table of the Word and in the Table of the Eucharist. Indeed, he comes to us alive whenever we participate in the celebration of the Eucharist. Like Mary, let us rejoice in this gift of God to us.

It is interesting to know that even though Simeon was old age, he trusted in the fulfillment of God's promises. He saw in the infant Jesus the fulfillment of that prophesy. In his old age, Simeon had desire for novelty. **What about us?** Are you aware that as Christians, we are supposed to be the dreamers of our time? This is because we can do all things through Christ who strengthens us *(Philippians 4: 13)*. Though the promise may be long, it takes an eye of faith to see its fulfillment even in its humble beginnings. "For there is still a vision for the appointed time; it speaks of the end and does not lie. If it seems to tarry, wait for it; it will surely come, it will not delay" (Habakkuk 2: 3). Even Mary who was the bearer of the good news was astonished at what was being said about the child and she kept all these things in her heart. Our God is a faithful God. He does not change like a shifting spanner; He neither slumbers nor sleeps. "For I the Lord do not change; therefore you, O children of Jacob have not perished. Ever since the days of your ancestors you have turned aside from my statutes and have not kept them. Return to me and I will return to you, says the Lord of host. But you say, how shall we return?" (Zechariah 3:6-7). Because He lives we can face tomorrow, because He alone possesses the key to our future and so we can trust him. Life is worth living just because he lives. The song writer says it all:

God sent His Son We
call Him Jesus He came
to die, heal and forgive

He lived and died

To buy my pardon

An empty grave is
there to prove that my
saviour lives

Because He lives

I can face tomorrow

Because He lives

All fear is gone

And now I know, yes I
know

He holds the future
and life is worth a
living just because He
lives.

CONCLUSION

In the Preface II of the Blessed Virgin Mary, the Church praises God with the words of Mary when she says,

"It is truly right and just, our duty and our salvation, to praise your mighty deeds in the exaltation of all the Saints, and especially as we celebrate the memory of the Blessed Virgin Mary, to proclaim your kindness as we echo her thankful hymn of praise. For truly to earth's ends you have done great things and extended your abundant mercy from age to age: when you looked on the lowliness of your handmaid, you gave us through her the author of our salvation, your Son, Jesus Christ our Lord..."

The above is what Mary heartily proclaims in the *Magnificat*. This is our love story; this is our tradition. We see how God consistently desires to draw fallen man closer and closer to himself. Concurrently, we see man's consistent attempt to go farther and farther away from God. The Prophet Hosea says:

> When Israel was a child, I loved him and out of Egypt I called my son. The more I called them, the more they went from me, they kept sacrificing to the Baals and offering incense to idols. Yet it was I who taught Ephraim to walk, I took them up in my arms; but they did not know that I healed them. I led them with cords of human kindness, with bands of love. I was to them like those who lifts infants to their cheeks. I bent down to them and fed them (Hosea 11:1-4).

The central attitude of Mary as expressed in the *Magnificat* is faith. Mary's being and the trajectory of her life are decisively shaped by the fact of her faith. The words of Elizabeth, " Blessed is she who believed..." (Luke 1:45) becomes the key word of Mariology.

Elizabeth's exclamation that " Blessed are you..." shows how God's promise to Abraham resounds once more at the beginning of the New Covenant as found concrete expression in Mary. God told Abraham: " I will make of you a great nation and I will bless you and make your name great so that you will be a blessing. I will bless those who bless you and the one who curses you, I will curse and in you all the families of the earth shall be bless" (Genesis 12:2-3). Mary, our Mother who recapitulates the faith of Abraham and brought it to its goal, is now called blessed. She has become the Mother of faith for all Christians through whom all generations and races of the earth obtain blessing. We place ourselves in this blessing when we praise her. We become part of it together with her, we become believers who magnify God because he dwells among us as "God with us", Jesus Christ, the true and only Redeemer of the World.

In the *Magnificat*, we see Mary reminding humanity of God's faithfulness to his promise to Abraham and how she has become that instrument for the fulfillment of that promise. That which God promised to Abraham is being fulfilled even today among us. In moments like this, we can sit back and reflect on how God has blessed us. We can count our blessings and name them one by one because God has fulfilled his promise even in our time. Indeed God makes things new in his time. The promise is for those who can see; those who can put their past behind them and move on with their lives. Like Blind bartimaeus (Mark 10: 46-52), let us ask God to make us see how He has blessed us and His promise of giving us a future and hope *(Jeremiah 29:14)* for what is the use of having eyes that cannot see?

MAY MARY OUR MOTHER THROUGH HER MATERNAL LOVE, HOLD OUR HANDS AND LEAD US CONTINUALLY TO HER SON.

The visit that occasioned the Magnificat

The meeting of the two women

BIBLIOGRAPHY

Hahn Scott, Hail Holy Queen: the Mother of God in the Word of God, Doubleday, New York, 2001.

Wiersbe Warren W., The Wierse Bible Commentary, David C., Cook, Colorado Springs, 2003.

Hans Urs Von Balthasar, Joseph Cardinal Ratzinger, Mary: The Church at the Source, Ignatian Press, San Francisco, 1980.

Lukefahr Luke, Christ's Mother and Ours: A Catholic Guide To Mary, Liguori, New York, 1998.

Jahn Curtis A., Exegesis and Sermon Study of Luke 1:46-55: The Magnificat, 1997.

The Roman Missal (English Translation), Catholic Book Publishing Corporation, New Jersey, 2011.

ZodhiatesSpiros TH.D, The Song of the Virgin: An Exposition of Luke 1:46-55, AMG Publishers, Chattanooga, 1985.

APPENDIX

Mary's Magnificat (Lk 1:46)	Old Testament
My soul glorifies the Lord	1 Sa 2:1 My heart rejoices in the LORD; in the LORD my horn is lifted high. Ps 34:2,3 My soul will boast in the Lord; let the afflicted hear and rejoice. Glorify the LORD with me; let us exalt His name together. Ps 103:1 Praise the LORD oh my soul; all my inmost being, praise His holy name.
v.47) and my spirit rejoices in God in my Saviour,	Ps 18:46b Exalted be God my Saviour! Isa 61:10I delight greatly in the LORD; my soul rejoices in my God. For He has clothed me with garments of salvation and arrayed me in a robe of righteousness.
v. 48a) for he has been mindful of the humble state of His servant.	Ps 138:6 Though the LORD is on high, He looks upon the lowly, but the proud He knows from afar.

v. 49a) for the Mighty One has done great things for me-	Ps 71:19 Your righteousness reaches to the skies, O God, you who have done great things. Who, O God, is like you?
v. 49b) Holy is His Name.	1 Sa 2:2 There is no one holy like the LORD; there is no one besides You. Ps 22:3 You are enthroned as the Holy One; you are the praise of Israel. Ps 71:22b I will sing praise to you with the Lyre, O Holy One of Israel. Ps 89:18 Indeed, our shield belongs to the LORD, our King to the Holy One of Israel. Ps 99:3 Let them praise your great and awesome Name-He is Holy. Ps 103:1b Praise His Holy Name.
v. 50) His mercy extends to those who fear Him, from generation to generation.	Ps 103:17 From everlasting to everlasting the LORD's love is with those who fear Him, and His righteousness with their children's children.
V. 51 a) He has performed	Ps 44:3 It was not by their sword that they won the land, nor did their arm bring them

mighty deeds with His arm;	victory; it was your right hand, your arm, and the light of your face, for you loved them.
	    Ps 77:14,15 You
	    the God who performs miracles; you display your power among the peoples. With your mighty arm you redeemed your people, the descendants of Jacob and Joseph.
	    Ps 98:1 Sing to the LORD a new song, for He has done marvelous things; His right hand His Holy arm have worked salvation for Him.

v. 51b) He has scattered those who are proud in their inmost thoughts.	1 Sam. 2:3 Do not keep talking so proudly or let your mouth speak such arrogance, for the LORD is a God who knows, and by him deeds are weighed.
	    2 Sam. 22:28 You save the humble, but your eyes are on the haughty to bring them low.
	    Ps 89:10 You crushed Rahab like one of the slam; with your strong arm you scattered your enemies.

v. 52a) He has brought	1Sam. 2:4Thebowsofthe warriorsarebroken (Pharaoh,

135

down rulers from their thrones	Sennacherib,Nebuchadnezzar, Belshazzar, etc)
v.53a) He has filled the hungry with good things	1 Sam. 2:5b but those who were hungry hunger no more. Ps 103:5 who satisfies your desires with good things. Ps 107:8,9 Let them give thanks to the LORD for his unfailing love and his wonderful deeds for men, for he satisfies the thirsty and fills the hungry with good things.
v. 53b) but He has sent the rich away empty.	1 Sam. 2:5 Those who were full hire themselves out for food.
vv. 54, 55a) He has helped his servant Israel, remembering to be merciful to Abraham and his descendants forever,	Ps 25:6 Remember, O LORD, your great mercy and love, for they are from of old. Ps 98:3 He has remembered His love and His faithfulness to the house of Israel. Ps 105:8-11 He remembers His covenant forever, the word He commanded, for a thousand generations, the covenant He made with Abraham, the oath he swore to Isaac. He confirmed to Jacob as

	a decree, to Israel as an everlasting covenant: "To you I will give the land of Canaan as the portion you will inherit." 　　Ps 136Aff. His love [mercy] endures forever
v.　　55b) even as He said to our fathers.	Gen. 12:1ff;22:15ff,; etc. Ps 147:19 He has revealed His word to Jacob, His laws and decrees to Israel. Mic 7:20 You will be true to Jacob, and show mercy to Abraham, as you pledged on oath to our fathers in days long ago.

GLOSSARY

Benedictus - it is also known as the Song of Zechariah or Canticle of Zachary. It is given in the Gospel according to Luke 1:68-79. It is one of the three Canticles in the opening chapters of this Gospel. It was a song of thanksgiving uttered by Zechariah on the occasion of the birth of John the Baptist.

Breviary- from the Latin Breviarium, it means an abridgment or a compendium.Next to the Holy Mass, the breviary is the most important prayer offered to God. It is offered by the Church and in the name of the Church, conferring multifold graces and blessings on those who pray it worthily, attentively and devoutly. It is by obligation prayed by Priests and religious.

Canticle- from the Latin canticulum, it is a hymn or song of praise taken from biblical texts other than the Psalms.

Compline- It is from the Latin Completorium meaning the completion of the working day. It is the final divine office of the day. It is also known as *Night Prayer*.

Intertestamental Period- this is the period from the book of Malachi at the end of our Old Testament to the opening of Matthew at the beginning of our New Testament comprising about 400yrs. This is also called " Silent Years" since prophecy in Israel was at a stand still.

Lauds- it is a divine office that takes place in the early morning hours and is one of the two major hours in the Liturgy of the Hours.

Legionary-it is the name given to a member of the Legion of Mary. The Legion of Mary is an association of Catholic Laity who serve the Church on a voluntary basis. It was founded in Dublin, Ireland, as a Roman Catholic Marian Movement by Frank Duff.

Liturgy of Hours- it refers to the official prayer of the Church offered at various times of the day in order to sanctify it. It is also called Divine Office

NuncDimittis-it is last in the historical sequence of the three great Canticles of the New Testament, the other two being the *Magnificat* and the Benedictus. It is the opening words of Simeon's song of praise on the occasion of the presentation of the infant Jesus in the Temple.

PAX ROMANA- it means peace from Rome. It is a name for all Catholic Students in tertiary institutions.

Pedagogic- it is the science and art of education, specifically instructional theory.

Theotokos- Mother of God

Vespers- it is the divine office that takes place in the evening. It is the second major hour of the day.

HYMNS

Magnificat

My soul now glorifies,
The Lord who is my
saviour Rejoice for
whom am I That God
has shown His favour

The world shall call me
blesses And ponder on
my story In me is
manifest God's
greatness and His
glory

For those who are his
friends And keep His
laws as holy His mercy
never ends for He
exalts the lowly

But by his power the
great The proud and
self-conceited The
kings who sit in state
Are humbled and de-
seated

*He feeds the starving
poor He guards his
holy nation*

*Fulfilling what He
swore Long since in
revelation Then glorify
with me The Lord who
is my savior One Holy
Trinity Forever and
forever*

HOLY VIRGIN BY GOD'S DECREE

1. Holy Virgin, by God's decree, You were called eternally; That he could give his Son to our race. Mary, we praise you, hail, full of grace. *Ref. Ave, ave, ave, Maria.*
2. By your faith and loving accord, As the handmaid of the Lord, You undertook God's plan to embrace. Mary we thank you, hail, full of grace.
3. Joy to God you gave and expressed, Of all women none more blessed, When in mankind your Son took his place. Mary, we love you, hail, full of grace.
4. Refuge for your children so weak, Sure protection all can seek. Problems of life you help us to face. Mary, we trust you, hail, full of grace.
5. To our needy world of today Love and beauty you portray, Showing the

path to Christ we must trace. Mary, our mother, hail, full of grace.

261 • Hail, Holy Queen Enthroned Above
Tune: SALVE REGINA CAELITUM (84 84 77 79)
Text: att. Hrm. Contractus (11th century)

PRAYER

Our lady of Fatima

Holy Mary Virgin of Fatima,

with renewed gratitude for your maternal presence we join our voice to that of all the generations who call you blessed.

We celebrate in you the works of God, who never tires of looking down with mercy upon humanity, afflicted with the wound of sin, to heal it and save it.

Accept with the benevolence of a Mother the act of consecration that we perform today with confidence, before this image of you that is so dear to us. We are certain that each of us is precious in your eyes and that nothing of all that lives in our hearts is unknown to you.

We let ourselves be touched by your most sweet regard and we welcome the consoling caress of your smile. Hold our life in your arms: bless and strengthen every desire for good; revive and nourish faith; sustain and enlighten hope; awaken and animate charity; guide all of us along the path of holiness.

Teach us your own preferential love for the little and the poor, for the excluded and the suffering, for sinners and the downhearted: bring everyone under your protection and entrust everyone to your beloved Son, Our Lord Jesus. Amen.

Pope Francis' prayer of Consecration of the world to the Immaculate Heart of Mary during the Feast day of our Lady of Fatima on October 13, 2013.